AMERICAN CIVIL LIBERTIES UNION

ACLU

HANDBOOKS FOR YOUNG AMERICANS

The Rights of
Racial Minorities

AMERICAN CIVIL LIBERTIES UNION

ACLU

HANDBOOKS FOR YOUNG AMERICANS

The Rights of Racial Minorities

LAUGHLIN McDONALD
john a. powell

with an introduction by Norman Dorsen

PUFFIN BOOKS

To my parents,
Marshall Powell, Jr., and Florice Powell,
and my kids,
Fon and Saneta DeVuono-powell

—j.p.

PUFFIN BOOKS
Published by the Penguin Group
Penguin Putnam Inc., 375 Hudson Street, New York, New York 10014, U.S.A.
Penguin Books Ltd, 27 Wrights Lane, London W8 5TZ, England
Penguin Books Australia Ltd, Ringwood, Victoria, Australia
Penguin Books Canada Ltd, 10 Alcorn Avenue, Toronto, Ontario, Canada M4V 3B2
Penguin Books (N.Z.) Ltd, 182-190 Wairau Road, Auckland 10, New Zealand

Penguin Books Ltd, Registered Offices: Harmondsworth, Middlesex, England

First published in the United States of America by Puffin Books,
a member of Penguin Putnam Inc., 1998

1 3 5 7 9 10 8 6 4 2

LIBRARY OF CONGRESS CATALOGING-IN-PUBLICATION DATA
McDonald, Laughlin.
The rights of racial minorities / Laughlin McDonald and john a. powell ; with an introduction by
Norman Dorsen.
p. cm. — (ACLU handbooks for young Americans)
Summary: Discussion and analysis of the rights of racial minorities, including historical
perspective and relevant court decisions.
Includes bibliographical references and index.
ISBN 0-14-037785-9 (pbk.)
1. Minorities—Legal status, laws, etc.—United States—Juvenile literature. 2. Race discrimina-
tion—Law and legislation—United States—Juvenile literature. [1. Minorities—Legal status,
laws, etc. 2. Racial discrimination—Law and legislation.] I. powell, john a. (John Anthony).
II. Dorsen, Norman. III. Title. IV. Series.
KF4755.Z9M38 1998 342.73'0873—dc21 97-36594 CIP AC

Printed in U.S.A.
Set in ITC Century Book

CONTENTS

FOREWORD

This guide sets forth the rights of racial minorities under the present law and offers suggestions on how they can be protected. It is one of a series of handbooks for young adults which is published in cooperation with the American Civil Liberties Union (ACLU).

This guide offers no assurances that the rights it discusses will be respected. The laws may change, and in some of the topics covered in these pages they change quite rapidly. An effort has been made to note those parts of the law where movement is taking place, but it is not always possible to predict accurately when the law *will* change.

Even if the laws remain the same, their interpretations by courts and administrative officials often vary. In a federal system such as ours, there is a built-in problem since state and federal law differ, not to mention the confusion between states. In addition, there are wide variations in how particular courts and administrative officials will interpret the same law at any given moment.

If you encounter what you consider to be a specific abuse of your rights, you should seek legal assistance. There are a number of agencies that may help you, among them ACLU affiliate offices, but bear in mind that the ACLU is a limited-purpose organization. In many communities, there are federally funded legal-service offices which provide assistance to persons who cannot afford the costs of legal representation. In general, the rights that the ACLU defends are freedom of inquiry and expression, due process of law, equal protection of the laws, and privacy. The authors in this series discuss other rights (even though they sometimes fall outside the ACLU's usual concern) in order to provide as much guidance as possible.

These publications carry the hope that Americans, informed of their rights, will be encouraged to exercise them. Through their exercise, rights are given life. If they are rarely used, they may be forgotten and violations may become routine.

It is of special importance that young people learn what their rights are and that there is such a thing as "rights"—individual liberties that the government, no matter how strong, must honor. Only a self-confident country can remain faithful to such a vision, and young people are the future of all countries, whether or not these recognize the value of rights to a thriving civilization. The handbooks in this series are designed to contribute to this goal.

Norman Dorsen
Stokes Professor,
New York University School of Law
President, ACLU 1976–1991

ACKNOWLEDGMENTS

For their work in helping to prepare the chapters on education, housing, federally assisted discrimination, and race-conscious remedies we would like to thank Justin Cummins, Vina Kay, Jennifer Nestle, Jeffrey Rutherford, Benjamin Weiss, Jim Hilbert, and James Lewis.

AUTHORS' NOTE

The content of this book focuses primarily on the civil-rights struggle and its development. Although *issues* of civil rights clearly impact all racial groups in the United States, the primary focus in the *development* of civil rights has been on African-Americans and white Americans. Most of our laws and public policy that relate to race have reflected this history.

This is not to say that the United States is a country of only two races. In fact, the U.S. is moving more toward a multiracial society. Yet despite the broad range of races in the U.S., on issues of civil rights, the black/white boundary has been the most definitive. Although as a society we are currently rethinking this boundary, the black/white paradigm still represents the core of both our legal development and the social model on issues of race.

In studying matters related to race, it is important to understand what race is and isn't. Early on, people argued that race was defined by genetics. Some scientists thought that the different races were different subspecies of human beings. This theory is called polygenetics. As you may know, polygenetics was later discredited. Today's science shows that all the races share a common genetic pool.

Although not a scientific fact, race remains an important social fact. Most scientists and social scientists today recognize that race is a social construct—that is, a way of looking at people based on tradition, custom, prevailing attitudes, and the law. It is in the social context that race is significant. Various groups of individuals in this country have been singled out for discriminatory treatment because of the color of their skin or their ancestry. As a society, we have used race to distribute cultural, societal, and economic resources and opportunities.

At various times during U.S. history, racial discrimination has been practiced against many different groups of people. Discrimination against African-Americans in particular, however, has had a unique impact on the development of civil-rights laws. The Thirteenth, Fourteenth, and Fifteenth Amendments were all enacted as a specific response to slavery and discrimination against African-Americans. Slavery and Jim Crow, or racial segregation that appeared after the Civil War, were directed primarily at African-Americans. For these reasons, this book focuses mainly on discrimination against African-Americans and the laws established to confront this racial discrimination.

This does not mean that civil-rights laws are limited to African-Americans. Any group may claim the right to equal protection under the Fourteenth Amendment—for instance, if it can show that it was singled out by the law for discriminatory treatment. State and federal statutes enacted to enforce the constitutional amendments also protect various groups from being discriminated against on the basis of race, color of skin, or national origin. The Voting Rights Act protects certain language minorities from discriminatory treatment in voting.

In this book then, we will be more concerned with how

race has and continues to function, than with its descriptive role. Because of this, we will focus on the civil-rights movement, which was developed primarily out of the black/white dynamic in the United States. There may be a need to reconsider this in the future, but for now we think this is an appropriate way to discuss the rights of minorities.

AMERICAN CIVIL LIBERTIES UNION

ACLU

HANDBOOKS FOR YOUNG AMERICANS

The Rights of
Racial Minorities

1

INTRODUCTION

American democracy was founded on a contradiction: that all people were equal but that human slavery was tolerable. The nation's belief in equality was written into the Declaration of Independence, which proclaimed that "all men are created equal." Its tolerance of slavery was contained in three provisions of the Constitution of 1787. One provision counted a slave as only three-fifths of a person in determining how many representatives each state was entitled to in the House of Representatives. A second prohibited Congress from abolishing the slave trade prior to the year 1808. The third provided for the return of fugitive slaves. The history of this nation has been in large measure the story—often violent, sometimes heroic, and always traumatic—of its attempts to reconcile its stated beliefs with its actual racial practices.

In 1857, the Supreme Court confronted the issue of whether slavery was lawful in the famous case of *Dred Scott v. Sanford*. Dred Scott, a slave, argued that he was entitled to his freedom because he had lived for a while in Illinois and the

Louisiana Territory, where slavery had been abolished. The court rejected his claim. It held that slaves were not citizens and were not entitled to sue for their freedom in the federal courts. The Court said that slaves and their descendants were "beings of an inferior order; and altogether unfit to associate with the white race, either in social or political relations; and so far inferior, that they had no rights which the white man was bound to respect; and that the negro might justly and lawfully be reduced to slavery for his benefit."[1]

Dred Scott further divided a nation already torn on the issue of slavery and foreshadowed the Civil War, which erupted four years later. Out of that war, in 1866, came the Thirteenth Amendment, which abolished the institution of human slavery. The Thirteenth Amendment did not, however, bring about racial equality.

Many of the states responded to abolition by enacting laws known as "black codes," which imposed upon blacks a status that was not much different from slavery. The black codes contained severe restrictions on the rights of freed blacks to own property, to travel, to sue in the courts, and to hold certain jobs.

Partly in response to the black codes, Congress enacted in 1866 a sweeping civil-rights act designed to confer full and equal citizenship upon blacks. The Fourteenth Amendment was ratified two years later, which among other things guarantees to all persons without regard to race the equal protection of the laws. The third and last of the post–Civil War constitutional amendments was the Fifteenth. It was ratified in 1870 and guarantees the equal right to vote.

The three Civil War amendments were reinforced by a number of congressional acts that sought to wipe out racial discrimination, regardless of whether it was supported by state law or by local custom. Congress required the former Confederate states to adopt new constitutions guaranteeing male suffrage (that is, the right to vote) without regard to race as a condition for reentering the Union. Federal troops were sent to the South to maintain order and supervise the voting registration of newly freed blacks. Despite widespread violence and intimidation by whites, blacks voted in substantial numbers and were elected to local, state, and national office.

This period in history, from the end of the Civil War until federal troops were withdrawn from the South in 1877, is known as Reconstruction. Had the Civil War amendments and the subsequent legislation been effectively enforced, some of the racial division and injustice that occurred over the next hundred years might have been avoided. But Reconstruction, as far as racial minorities were concerned, turned out to be a failure.

Within only a few years after its passage, the Supreme Court held much of the legislation designed to enforce the Civil War amendments unconstitutional. The Court also severely limited the application of the amendments themselves. Civil-rights legislation was further weakened by Congress, which repealed major portions of the remaining laws.

After the withdrawal of federal troops, the Confederate states were left free to deal with racial matters as they saw fit. They opted for legalized racial segregation, known as "Jim Crow." They also kept blacks from voting through such discriminatory devices as literacy tests and the poll tax for registering and voting. By the turn of the century, blacks—though no longer enslaved—were relegated to the status of second-class citizens.

The inevitable result of Jim Crow and racial discrimination was injustice, bitterness, and violence. There were some five thousand reported lynchings in the United States after 1859 and full-blown race riots across the nation—in New York in 1900; in Springfield, Ohio, in 1904; in Statesboro and Atlanta in

1906; in Greensburg, Indiana, in 1906; and in Brownsville, Texas, and Springfield, Illinois, in 1908. But the forces for racial change in the United States were never entirely stilled.

In 1905, responding to lynchings and racial discrimination, W.E.B. DuBois and others, many of whom were former abolitionists, met at Niagara Falls, New York, and founded the Niagara Protest movement. It was DuBois who wrote prophetically that "the problem of the twentieth century is the problem of the color-line."[2] Later, in 1909 and 1910, the founders of the Niagara Movement formed the National Association for the Advancement of Colored People (NAACP) and adopted an agenda for racial reform that served as a blueprint during the next 50 years.

Other forces were at work which contributed to a climate of racial change in America. Blacks began to migrate in substantial numbers to the North in search of jobs, where many of them voted for the first time and experienced life free of some of the formal restraints of segregation. Blacks also served in World War I, although in Jim Crow units. When they returned home, they began to demand equal status in the democracy they had fought to preserve. The federal government appointed a number of blacks to key administrative positions, and in 1939 Congress created a Civil Rights Section in the Department of Justice.

American intervention in World War II had a further, profound effect on race relations in the United States. It was morally indefensible to make war against Nazi racism in Europe and defend white supremacy at home. The United States also joined the United Nations, whose charter called for equal rights without regard to race, sex, or religion. Many Americans felt that if the charter and American involvement in the United Nations were to have real meaning, the country had to reassess its domestic racial policies.

In 1944, a Swedish economist named Gunnar Myrdal published a highly influential book on race relations in the United States, *An American Dilemma*. He concluded that the status of blacks was not the result of natural inferiority, as the defenders of segregation claimed, but of racial discrimination. Blacks were trapped in a circular self-fulfilling prophecy: discrimination had reduced them to second-class status, but that status was in turn used to justify racial discrimination.

President Truman created a Committee on Civil Rights in 1946 to determine ways to secure equal rights. Two years later, he desegregated the armed forces. In spite of predictions of bloodshed and race riots, desegregation proceeded without incident.

The Supreme Court, reflecting a thaw in racial attitudes, also began slowly and sporadically to chip away at Jim Crow. In a series of cases it declared a number of laws and practices unconstitutional: a city ordinance requiring racial segregation in neighborhood housing; the enforcement by state courts of provisions in deeds to real estate that prohibited resale to minorities; and racial segregation in interstate transportation (in trains, buses, etc., that carry passengers from one state to another).

The most dramatic breakthrough in racial reform came in 1954 in *Brown v. Board of Education*, which involved state laws requiring racial segregation in public schools. The Court held that separate educational facilities were "inherently unequal" and that Jim Crow schools deprived blacks of equal protection guaranteed by the Fourteenth Amendment.[3] The *Brown* decision marked the beginning of the end of Jim Crow. The decade following *Brown*, with its renewed promise of racial equality, has aptly been called the Second Reconstruction.

But if *Brown* held out hope, it also drew massive resistance from states that stood to be most affected by it. School desegregation was not in fact significantly implemented until the 1970s, more than fifteen years after the *Brown* opinion.

In response to an increasing popular demand for equal rights, Congress enacted major civil-rights legislation during the 1960s. These modern statutes protect racial minorities against most forms of public and private discrimination in employment, housing, public accommodations, programs supported by federal dollars, education, voting, and the administration of civil and criminal laws.

Our constitutional and legislative systems provide the means to ensure equality and to eradicate the continuing effects of past discrimination accumulated over more than two centuries. But laws do not enforce themselves. The challenge to all of us is to make the laws work, to ensure that the *principle* that all persons are created equal becomes a *reality*.

2

VOTING

During the early history of the United States, voting was typically limited to white male property owners over the age of 21. After the Civil War, the Confederate states were required to guarantee universal male suffrage without regard to race as a condition for reentering the Union. With the adoption in 1870 of the Fifteenth Amendment, the equal right of men to vote without regard to race was guaranteed nationwide, at least in theory. (Women did not get the right to vote until adoption of the Nineteenth Amendment in 1920.)

CONSTITUTIONAL PROTECTION OF VOTING RIGHTS

What kind of discrimination in voting is prohibited by the Fifteenth Amendment?

The Fifteenth Amendment prohibits purposeful discrimination in voting at all levels of the political process by federal, state, and local officials on the basis of race, color, or previous condition of servitude. The amendment pertains to sophisticated as well as simple-minded forms of discrimination, such as requiring people to take a deliberately difficult and confusing test before registering or simply closing the registration office whenever minorities try to register. While the amendment was enacted as a limitation on public officials, the acts of private individuals are also unconstitutional where they perpetuate or act as a substitute for official discrimination. For example, political parties, even though they are private organizations, may not exclude people on the basis of race from membership or from voting in their primaries because the primaries are a central part of the electoral process.

Was the Fifteenth Amendment effectively enforced after its ratification in 1870?

Far from it. Congress enacted a variety of voting laws during Reconstruction to enforce the Fifteenth Amendment, but its good intentions were nullified by the other branches of the federal government. Congress required election officials to give all citizens the same opportunity to vote. It made it a federal crime to violate state laws governing the election of federal officials, to interfere with a citizen's right to vote, or to commit fraudulent acts in connection with registering voters or counting ballots. Congress also established a system of federal supervisors of elections. None of these laws was adequately enforced, and some of them were declared unconstitutional by the Supreme Court. Then, in 1894, Congress itself repealed many of the post–Civil War voting laws, including those dealing with federal supervision of state elections.

What was the consequence of the lack of enforcement?

Predictably, the consequence was the disfranchisement of African-Americans—that is, they were deprived of the right to vote. Immediately after the Civil War, despite widespread intimidation and violence by whites, blacks registered and voted in substantial numbers in the states where they had formerly been denied the ballot. Many blacks were elected to office. But minority participation in the elective process was generally possible only because of the presence of federal troops dispatched under various Reconstruction laws.

After Reconstruction ended in 1877, the disfranchisement of blacks began in earnest, and the promise of equal voting rights held out by the Fifteenth Amendment faded. A common method of discouraging blacks from voting was to make the elective process more difficult. White legislators gave free rein to their imaginations in burdening the right to vote with onerous requirements.

The main work of disfranchisement was accomplished through a series of state constitutional conventions. The first was held in Mississippi in 1890. Its stated purpose was to deprive blacks of the right to vote. A favorite way of excluding minorities from voting adopted by the Southern states was the literacy test. The test required a person to read and write a portion of the Constitution as a condition for registering. The literacy test was racially neutral on its face, but it was administered in a way that excluded blacks, but not whites, from voting. To make sure that illiterate whites were not disfranchised, alternatives to literacy were provided. A person could register if he could "understand and interpret" the Constitution, owned property, or had "good character." Many states enacted "grandfather clauses," which excused persons previously registered, and their descendants, from having to comply with any additional registration requirements. Few blacks could qualify for registration under the grandfather clauses, since blacks were almost never previously allowed to vote. The poll tax was another way of limiting the right to vote. The tax was, in

essence, a fee for the privilege of voting and fell with disproportionate impact upon poor blacks.

One of the most effective ways of denying political participation to minorities was through the use of the "all-white" primary. Membership in the Democratic party and voting in the
party's primary were limited to whites. Since political parties
were groups of private individuals, they appeared to be beyond
the reach of the Fifteenth Amendment. And because nomina-
tion in the Democratic primary was tantamount to election to
office in the states that used the all-white primary, African-
Americans, even those who were registered, were shut out
from the elective process.

Voter-registration figures reveal the effectiveness of post-
Reconstruction disfranchisement. In Louisiana in 1896, there
were 130,334 blacks registered to vote. In 1900, there were
only 5,320. In Mississippi, 70 percent of the black voting-age
population was registered to vote in 1867. By 1899, the figure
had dropped to 9 percent. It is no exaggeration to say that, at
the turn of the century, blacks no longer participated in a
meaningful way in the political life of the United States.

**Did any of the laws designed to implement the Fifteenth
Amendment survive Reconstruction?**

Yes. Some of the Reconstruction voting laws have survived: a
statute protecting the right to vote without regard to race or
color; two laws making those who interfere with protected
rights (for example, the right to vote) liable for money damages in civil, or private, lawsuits brought by the victims of the
discrimination; and two statutes imposing criminal penalties
(imprisonment or fines) on persons who hinder others in their
attempts to vote. Even these surviving laws were limited in
their scope and, until recently, were infrequently used. Some
laws were used to prevent election fraud but were rarely used

to protect against racial discrimination in exercise of the right to vote. Other laws were used in banning all-white primaries but seldom to attack other forms of discrimination in voting.

Was the Fifteenth Amendment eventually revived?

Yes, but only gradually. It was not until 1915, 45 years after its ratification, that the amendment was actually used by the Supreme Court to invalidate a discriminatory election procedure. The Court declared the grandfather clause unconstitutional because its only purpose was to exclude blacks from voting. But in the same case, the Court approved the use of discriminatory literacy tests for voting. In the Court's view, the use of literacy tests was a local matter and not subject to federal review.

Has Congress taken any action since Reconstruction to protect the voting rights of minorities?

Yes. In 1957, Congress passed the first civil-rights act since the Civil War. The act established the six-member bipartisan (meaning it included people from both the Democratic and the Republican parties) Commission on Civil Rights and gave it the duty of gathering information on discrimination in voting. It also prohibited interference with voting in federal elections. It authorized the attorney general (the chief law officer of the U.S.) to bring lawsuits to protect voting rights, and set out procedures for holding in criminal contempt, or punishing, those who disobeyed court orders ending discrimination by making them pay fines or sentencing them to jail. The act was amended in 1960 to authorize federal referees to investigate voting discrimination and to register qualified voters.

Four years later, Congress enacted the Civil Rights Act of 1964. It provided, among other things, that black registration be based upon the same voter qualifications that traditionally

11

had been applied to whites; that any literacy or other test for voting be given entirely in writing; that unimportant errors in answering test questions not be made the basis for denying registration; and that a person with a sixth-grade education was presumed to be literate.

The 1957, 1960, and 1964 acts were often used effectively to deal with specific voting-rights violations, but they did not cause much increase in minority voter registration. They were also hard to enforce because they relied primarily on time-consuming lawsuits brought by the attorney general or injured parties. In 1965, Congress adopted an entirely new approach to voter legislation. It passed the Voting Rights Act, which suspended the tests that had been used to exclude minorities from registration and required any new voting procedures to be approved by federal officials. The Voting Rights Act is the most important law on the books protecting voting rights. It is discussed in more detail below.

Congress also enacted the National Voter Registration Act in 1993 after finding that cumbersome state registration laws had depressed voter participation, particularly that of racial minorities. The act requires the states to adopt uniform, simplified procedures for registering to vote in elections for federal offices and to allow registration by mail and at various state agencies.

Can political parties still discriminate or exclude racial minorities from membership or voting in primaries?

No. Even though political parties are private organizations, the Supreme Court has held that they are an important part of the public process of choosing elected officials. Discrimination by a political party is not just a private matter but amounts to unconstitutional state action.

Can proof of payment of a poll tax be required for voting in federal or state elections?

No. The poll, or head, tax was never regarded as an effective way of raising money on which to operate the government. Like the literacy test, requiring proof of payment of a poll tax was simply a way to keep blacks from voting. Nonetheless, the Supreme Court initially ruled in 1937 that proof of payment of the tax was constitutional. Numerous attempts were subsequently made to abolish the poll tax through federal legislation. The tax was finally banned in federal elections in 1964 by ratification of the Twenty-fourth Amendment. Two years later, the Supreme Court, reversing its earlier decision, declared the poll tax in state elections to be a violation of the Fourteenth Amendment. The wealth of a voter or the ability to pay a fee was not a proper basis for determining who could vote.

Are literacy or education tests for registering and voting constitutional?

No test which requires registrants to read and explain the state or federal Constitution is constitutional if it is used to exclude minorities from voting. Under such circumstances, the test is simply a trap to keep even the most brilliant person from voting. (Literacy and similar tests for voting are also banned by the Voting Rights Act of 1965.)

Is discrimination or intimidation by private individuals against racial minorities in registering and voting unlawful?

Yes. Although neither the Fourteenth nor Fifteenth Amendments prohibits private acts of discrimination, article I, section 4 of the Constitution gives Congress authority to regulate federal elections and to pass laws prohibiting private discrimination in registering and voting for federal officials. In applying these laws, the courts have banned assaults and threats by private individuals against minority registrants, as well as different forms of economic coercion.

In one case from Tennessee in 1961, blacks who registered, and whites who assisted them, were blacklisted and denied credit and the right to buy goods by local white businessmen. Tenant farmers and sharecroppers who were blacklisted were evicted by their white landowners. In a lawsuit filed to stop the intimidation, a court ordered the businessmen and the landowners to stop interfering with the rights of blacks to register and vote.

What other kinds of intentional discrimination have been struck down under the Constitution and federal voting laws?

Just about every kind imaginable. Racial discrimination in voting has taken many forms. It has included such crude measures as segregated polling places; segregated voter-registration procedures; the discriminatory literacy test; purges of blacks from registration lists; the requirement that the race of every candidate for elective office appear on the ballot; the arrest and prosecution of blacks conducting voter-registration drives; and the disfranchisement of persons convicted of crimes that blacks were thought more likely to commit than whites. More subtle practices included slowdowns in processing minority registration applications and the resignation from office of state officials (leaving plaintiffs in voting-rights lawsuits with no one to sue). All of these practices have been held to be unlawful.

A classic example of racial discrimination in voting, at once crude and ingenious, involved the city of Tuskegee, Alabama, in 1960. It redrew its city limits into an irregular 28-sided figure. The result of the alteration was to remove all but four or five of the city's black voters, but not a single white voter. The Supreme

Court had little trouble in finding that the new city lines were discriminatory and in violation of the Fifteenth Amendment.

Are so-called ballot integrity or security programs permissible?

These programs, conducted by political groups to purge persons from the voter rolls who are suspected of being improperly registered, are not permissible if the purpose of the program is to remove minorities from the voter rolls or to intimidate them from voting. In a 1986 Louisiana case, the Republican party did a mailing of approximately 300,000 letters targeted to minority voters. The envelopes were marked "Do Not Forward." Those that were returned were sent to local county registrars with a demand that the voters be purged because they were not residents or were illegally registered. Over 95 percent of those sought to be purged were black. The court concluded that the party had not adequately investigated whether the voters were legally registered. It held that the ballot security program was nothing more than an insidious scheme by the Republican party to remove blacks from the voting rolls and was in violation of the Fifteenth Amendment.

What is minority vote dilution?

Minority vote dilution, as distinguished from vote denial, is the impairment of the equal opportunity of minority voters to participate in the political process and to elect candidates of their choice. Even where the right to register and vote is freely available, a minority's voting strength may be diluted in a variety of ways: through at-large elections; by reapportionment plans that fragment (crack), submerge (stack), or concentrate (pack) the minority population; through use of numbered posts, staggered terms of office, and majority vote requirements; by laws prohibiting single-shot voting; by discriminatory annexations; and by the abolition of elected or appointed offices. The various ways of minimizing the impact of minority voting strength will be discussed in more detail later in this chapter.

Is the dilution of minority voting strength prohibited by the Constitution?

Yes. The equal-protection clause of the Fourteenth Amendment prohibits the dilution of minority voting strength. The prohibition has its roots in the "one person, one vote" decisions of the Supreme Court, which held that voting districts within a jurisdiction had to contain approximately the same numbers of people. In subsequent cases, the Court held that voting strength could be unconstitutionally diluted on the basis of race as well as population inequality.

How is unconstitutional vote dilution proved?

To prove a constitutional violation, a person must show that a voting practice was adopted or is being maintained with a racially discriminatory purpose. A challenger must also show that the practice has at least some discriminatory effect.

A discriminatory purpose need not be shown by direct evidence, such as statements by elected officials that they intended to discriminate by adopting a particular voting procedure. A purpose to discriminate may be inferred from the relevant facts and circumstances of a given case.

The courts typically consider a broad range of factors in determining if minority voting strength is diluted: (1) a history of discrimination; (2) the existence of racially exclusive groups that endorse, or slate, candidates; (3) cultural and language barriers; (4) depressed minority-voter registration; (5) lack of responsiveness by elected officials to the needs of the minority community; (6) the extent to which minorities have been elected to office; and (7) the use of election devices that enhance

vote dilution, such as numbered posts and majority vote requirements, which are discussed in more detail below. Based upon
the "totality of the circumstances," a court must decide whether
there has been a constitutional violation and whether minorities
have less opportunity than other residents to participate in the
political processes and to elect representatives of their choice.

Is the prohibition against minority vote dilution contrary to the democratic notion of majority rule?

No. A fundamental principle embodied in the amendments to
the Constitution is that there are limitations on majority control and power. For example, the Supreme Court held that segregation in the public schools was in violation of the
Fourteenth Amendment, even though a majority of residents in
the South were no doubt in favor of it. Majority rule is ignored
elsewhere in the Constitution, for example, in the provisions
requiring a vote of two-thirds of the members of the Senate to
remove the president from office and to ratify treaties. Under
our system, minorities have rights, including the right to participate equally in the political process.

How can at-large elections dilute minority voting strength?

When voting is at-large, all the voters in a jurisdiction elect all
the officials. The majority, if it votes as a bloc, can choose all the
officeholders, thereby depriving a minority of the opportunity to
elect any representatives of its choice. At-large elections are a
"winner-take-all" system that favors the numerical majority.

How can a majority-vote requirement dilute minority voting strength?

When a majority-vote requirement is in effect, a candidate is
required to get 50 percent plus one of the votes cast. If no can-

didate gets a majority, a runoff is held between the two highest vote-getters. Under a plurality system, the candidate who gets the most votes, even if less than a majority, wins. A majority-vote requirement gives an advantage to a racial majority. Suppose that one black and several whites were to run for the same office in a majority white jurisdiction. If voting were along racial lines, it is very possible that the white votes would be split among the white candidates and that the black would get a plurality of the votes cast. If the black candidate fell short of a majority—which would be likely since blacks would be a minority of voters—there would be a runoff election. In the runoff, the white voters could regroup behind the sole white candidate and elect that person to office.

Aside from its direct effect, a majority-vote requirement can discourage minority candidates from seeking office in majority white jurisdictions. Where voting is along racial lines, minority candidates could not generally expect to get enough white crossover votes to win and consequently often don't run for office.

How can numbered posts and staggered terms of office dilute minority voting strength?

Numbered posts and staggered terms are often used in elections for multimember bodies such as city councils, county commissions, or state legislatures. When terms are staggered they begin and end at different times. For example, half the members of a county commission might be elected in even-numbered years and the other half in odd-numbered years. Under a numbered-post system, candidates run for individual seats, or posts, rather than simply for a given number of vacancies. Numbered posts and staggered terms isolate candidates in head-to-head contests. Where voting is polarized, they allow the majority greater control over the outcome of elections.

How do anti–single shot laws dilute minority voting strength?

Single-shot or bullet voting occurs when a minority concentrates its votes on one or a few minority candidates. For example, if five seats for a city council were up for election, and if there were no numbered-post or majority-vote requirements, a minority might be able to overcome bloc voting by the majority and elect someone to office by voting only for one candidate. If an anti–single shot, or full slate, rule were in effect, voters would be required to vote for all five seats in order for their votes to count. Anti–single shot laws force minorities to vote for opposition candidates and destroy the effectiveness of bullet voting.

What are cracking, stacking, and packing?

Cracking, stacking, and packing are techniques used in redistricting to minimize minority political influence. Cracking is fragmenting an area that has a heavy concentration of minority population and dispersing it among several districts so that no district is majority-minority. Stacking is combining concentrations of minority population with larger concentrations of majority population, again to ensure that no district is majority-minority. Packing is concentrating the minority population into as few districts as possible to minimize the number of districts that are minority-majority.

Can a jurisdiction take race into account in redistricting?

Yes. One of the basic purposes of redistricting is to allocate the power to govern among the various groups that make up the electorate, whether the groups are political, socioeconomic, occupational, regional, ethnic, or racial. Legislators are also aware of race as a factor that influences voting behavior and take it into account in drawing district lines. As a practical matter, it would be impossible for legislators to ignore race in the redistricting process.

Can a jurisdiction take race into account in drawing district lines to enhance minority voting strength?

Yes—to remedy a violation of federal law, to avoid a violation of federal law, or to overcome the effects of racial bloc voting and past discrimination.

Are there any limitations on the extent to which a jurisdiction can consider race in enhancing minority voting strength?

Yes. A redistricting plan designed to enhance minority voting strength is suspect under the Fourteenth Amendment if race was the predominant factor in the redistricting process and if the jurisdiction subordinated all of its traditional redistricting principles to race. Under such circumstances, the plan can be used only if it promotes a compelling state interest and is narrowly tailored.

Examples of compelling state interests would be remedying or avoiding a violation of federal law or overcoming the effects of past discrimination. A plan would be narrowly tailored if it made no more use of race than was necessary and did not dilute the voting strength of non-minority voters.

How are the Fourteenth and Fifteenth Amendments enforced?

The Fourteenth and Fifteenth Amendments are enforced by lawsuits filed by the victims of discrimination and by the attorney general. The federal government also has the power to prosecute violations of criminal laws protecting voting rights.

What remedies are available for constitutional violations?

As a general matter, any remedy must be full and complete. The scope of the remedy will thus depend upon the nature and extent of the violation. Remedies for violations in voting cases include court orders ending the discrimination; retroactive relief, such as the setting aside of election results; the establishment of new election procedures; and awards of attorneys' fees and damages.

Can a person be made to disclose his or her race as a condition for registering to vote?

Yes, if state law requires it. Many states require persons to list their race on voter-registration forms. If the forms are not fully completed, registration may be denied. None of these compulsory disclosure laws have been held unconstitutional in themselves by the Supreme Court. However, their discriminatory misuse to deny registration only to noncomplying racial minorities, or the misuse of the information itself to segregate or purge blacks on voter lists, would be unlawful. Requiring disclosure of race serves a number of legitimate purposes. It helps the government in formulating and evaluating legislative programs to assist minorities. It also aids the courts in fashioning remedies for past discrimination.

In a related context, the Voting Rights Act authorizes the census to conduct surveys and compile statistics on the extent to which racial minorities are registered and have voted. The main purpose of the surveys is to assist Congress in evaluating the effectiveness of voting-rights laws and the need for additional legislation. Some persons object to supplying the government with racial information because of their fear that it will be misused. Others believe that notions of race and ethnic origin are loose and unscientific and constitute an invasion of privacy. To meet these concerns, the act provides that no person may be compelled to disclose race, color, or national origin in response to any census survey. To further ensure privacy, the act makes it a crime to misuse the survey data.

THE VOTING RIGHTS ACT OF 1965

What are the basic provisions of the Voting Rights Act of 1965?

The Voting Rights Act of 1965 abolished tests or devices for voting which had been used to disfranchise racial minorities. The terms "test" and "device" include literacy tests, educational requirements, and good-character tests. They also include exclusively English language registration and election procedures (which can make it difficult or impossible for those who are not fluent in English to vote) where a single language minority comprises more than 5 percent of the voting-age population of the jurisdiction. A second provision of the act, section 5, requires certain jurisdictions, known as "covered" jurisdictions, to gain approval, or preclearance, from federal authorities before implementing changes in voting practices. The jurisdiction has the burden of proving that any proposed voting change does not have the purpose or effect of abridging the right to vote on account of race, color, or membership in a language minority. The act also provides for federal voter registrars and observers, absentee balloting in presidential elections, and bilingual ballots for language minorities. Section 2 of the act provides that voting practices are unlawful if they result in discrimination.

Is it necessary to prove a discriminatory purpose to establish a violation of section 2?

No. When it amended the Voting Rights Act in 1982, Congress provided that a violation of section 2 could be established by showing either the discriminatory purpose or the discriminatory result of a challenged practice. Congress rejected exclusive reliance upon intent for three basic reasons: it was unnecessarily divisive because it required plaintiffs to prove that local officials were racists; the burden of proof was too difficult; and it asked "the wrong question." The "right question" was whether minorities had an equal opportunity to participate in the political process and elect candidates of their choice.

Is the Voting Rights Act ban on literacy and education tests for voting nationwide?

Yes. Literacy or other tests were suspended by the Voting Rights Act initially only in those states in which the tests had been designed to disfranchise racial minorities. Later, the ban was made nationwide and permanent by amendments to the act in 1970 and 1975. The Supreme Court held the nationwide ban constitutional after concluding that literacy tests had reduced voter participation in a discriminatory manner throughout the country.

Do the preclearance procedures of section 5 also apply nationwide?

No. Section 5 covers only those states, or parts of a state, which used a test or device for voting and in which voter participation was depressed. The attorney general and the director of the census are responsible for determining which areas are covered by section 5.

Which jurisdictions are covered by section 5?

The following states are covered by section 5: Alabama, Alaska, Arizona, Georgia, Louisiana, Mississippi, South Carolina, Texas, and Virginia. Portions of the following states are also covered: California (4 counties), Florida (5 counties), Michigan

(2 towns), New Hampshire (10 towns), New York (3 counties), North Carolina (40 counties), and South Dakota (2 counties).

Is coverage under section 5 permanent?

No. Congress enacted section 5 in 1965 as a temporary, five-year measure. It was designed to combat the extraordinary defiance of equal voting rights in certain sections of the country, and because of the failure of litigation to end discrimination. Congress extended section 5 in 1970, 1975, and 1982 after concluding that it was still needed to protect minority voting rights. The statute is now scheduled to expire in the year 2007.

Is coverage under section 5 of real significance?

Yes. Coverage under section 5 is enormously significant. It means that no change in voting procedures in a covered jurisdiction may be implemented unless the change has first been cleared to ensure that it does not have the purpose or effect of discriminating on account of race, color, or membership in a language minority. Section 5 provides an effective safeguard against enactment of new forms of discrimination.

What kinds of changes in voting are covered by section 5?

The Supreme Court has generally given section 5 a broad interpretation. Changes required to be precleared include the relocation of a polling place, annexations (even of vacant land), staggering of terms of office, majority-vote requirements, changes to single-member or multimember districts, abolition of elective or appointive offices, changing of precinct lines, redistricting, changes in filing fees or other candidacy requirements, a change in the date of an election, and a requirement that a county judge pay the salaries of persons in his or her office who had previously been paid by the county commission. Even a rule adopted by a county school board that its employees take unpaid leaves of absence while campaigning for elective office was held to be a change in voting requiring preclearance.

How is preclearance obtained?

Preclearance may be obtained in two ways. The change may be submitted administratively to the attorney general. She has 60 days within which to make an objection (or 120 days if she requests, or a jurisdiction submits, additional information). If the attorney general does not object, the proposed change may be implemented. If the attorney general objects, the change is rendered null and void, and the existing law remains in effect.

The second method by which a jurisdiction may obtain preclearance, whether or not submission has been made to the attorney general, is to bring a lawsuit in the federal district court in the District of Columbia. If the court rules that the change does not have a discriminatory purpose or effect, it can be implemented. Otherwise, the change may not take effect. Because of the time and expense of legal proceedings, most jurisdictions submit their proposed changes in voting to the attorney general for preclearance.

Once a submission is made, how does the attorney general or the federal court determine whether to grant clearance?

The standard for preclearance is whether the proposed change has the purpose or effect of denying or abridging the right to vote on account of race, color, or membership in a language minority. Discriminatory purpose under section 5 is the sort of harmful purpose that would support a constitutional challenge. Discriminatory effect under section 5 has been defined as retrogression, that is, where a change will make members of the minority group worse off than they were before the change. In determining retrogression, the attorney general and the courts normally compare the proposed change with the practice in effect at the time of the submission.

Some changes in voting, such as those that increase the hours for voter registration, would obviously be unobjectionable. Other changes, such as those that make registration and voting more difficult, would be denied preclearance. If the attorney general or the court cannot determine whether a change might have a prohibitive effect, preclearance must still be denied. Under section 5, there is a presumption that a submission is discriminatory. If the submitting authority cannot rebut the presumption, the proposed change cannot be implemented.

The allocation of the burden of proof to the submitting jurisdiction was a critical and innovative feature of section 5. It has proved to be a substantial curb to the introduction of new, discriminatory voting procedures. Many section 5 submissions are decided based on the failure of the jurisdiction to carry its burden of proof rather than on a positive finding of discrimination.

Are changes that increase minority participation in the elective process—but do so only partially— objectionable under section 5?

Generally, no. A change in election procedures that removes some but not all barriers to voting ordinarily will not violate section 5. But even a change that did not make minorities worse off than they were before (that is, was nonretrogressive) would violate section 5 if its purpose was to limit minority political participation.

Is there anything to keep a covered jurisdiction from ignoring section 5 and implementing changes in voting that have not been precleared?

Yes. The attorney general or any person affected by a change in voting can file a lawsuit in the local federal district court for an order prohibiting the jurisdiction from using an uncleared change. If the jurisdiction is covered and the change affects voting but has not been precleared, the court must prohibit further use of the change. The court has no jurisdiction to determine whether the change violates section 5. This issue can be resolved only by the attorney general or the federal court in the District of Columbia. Appeals from the decisions of local courts go directly to the Supreme Court.

The Voting Rights Act also makes it a crime to fail to comply with preclearance. Noncompliance has been widespread, but no one has ever been prosecuted for such an offense, presumably because of the existence of other, more effective ways of enforcing section 5 and the reluctance of the federal government to prosecute local officials.

If an uncleared change has been implemented, can the courts grant retroactive relief?

Yes. If an uncleared change has been implemented, the court must not only enjoin its further use but fashion a remedy to undo the harm caused by the failure to comply. For example, the court might shorten the terms of office of those elected under an unprecleared redistricting plan and order new elections under the preexisting plan. Or the court might allow the jurisdiction an opportunity to seek preclearance of the new plan and grant further relief only if preclearance were denied.

What is the standard for proving vote dilution under the results test of amended section 2?

The legislative history of the 1982 amendments sets out factors taken from the prior case law that courts should ordinarily consider in section 2 cases. The factors include racial bloc voting; a history of discrimination; depressed levels of minority employment, income, and education; few minorities elected to office; the presence of formal or informal organizations that endorse candidates for public office; the existence of racial campaign appeals; and the use of devices that enhance discrimination, such as numbered posts and a majority vote requirement. Other factors that might be relevant are a lack of responsiveness by elected officials to the needs of the minority community and a discriminatory or irrational policy underlying the use of the challenged practice.

Has the Supreme Court approved the use of the results test in section 2 cases?

Yes. The Court first applied section 2 to invalidate multimember districts in North Carolina's 1982 legislative redistricting. The Court established a three-part test for determining when at-large voting violated the results standard. First, the minority must be able to show that it is sufficiently large and geographically compact to constitute a majority in one or more single-member districts. Second, it must show that it is politically cohesive or tends to vote as a bloc. Third, it must show that the majority votes as a bloc usually to defeat the minority's preferred candidates. Where these three factors are shown, the court must then determine whether, based on other relevant facts and circumstances, a challenged practice deprives the minority of the equal opportunity to participate in the political process and elect candidates of its choice. It would be an unusual case in which minorities proved the three section 2 factors but failed to win on the merits of their vote-dilution claim.

What is bloc voting?

The Supreme Court adopted a simple, common-sense definition of bloc voting. Bloc voting exists where black voters and white voters vote differently. Bloc voting that is legally significant—*i.e.*, that will sustain a section 2 violation—exists where a white bloc vote normally will defeat the combined strength of minority plus any white crossover votes.

How is bloc voting proved?

Bloc voting can be proved through statistical analysis showing the relationship between the race of voters and the race of candidates. Bloc voting can also be shown by the testimony of experienced politicians who are familiar with voting patterns and by such factors as few minority candidates or elected officials and a history of discrimination.

Is it necessary to show that voters are motivated by race?

No. It is enough to show that voters of different races vote differently. What is important under section 2 is voter behavior, not its explanations.

What kind of voting practices are subject to challenge under section 2?

Section 2 applies to any practice that affects voting. That includes electoral structures such as at-large elections and redistricting plans, as well as practices that occur on a one-time basis. The courts have generally given section 2 a broad construction, and have held that such practices as the failure to appoint blacks as poll officials, the requirement of separate registration for city and county elections, and the wording of a question on the ballot calling for an increase in taxes were subject to challenge under section 2.

Can a single-member districting plan be challenged under section 2 on the ground that it dilutes minority voting strength?

Yes. The courts apply the same analysis to single-member district plans as to at-large elections in determining a section 2 violation.

What kind of remedies are required for section 2 violations?

Congress did not specify any particular remedies for violations of the statute. Instead, it said a court has the duty to fashion relief so that it completely remedies the dilution of minority voting strength and fully provides an equal opportunity for minorities to participate and to elect candidates of their choice.

In cases involving at-large elections, the courts have generally ordered single-member districts as a remedy. They have also required that a fair number of the districts be majority-minority. Successful plaintiffs may be entitled to special elections, orders ending the discrimination, and awards of damages and attorneys' fees.

Are plans that contain some combination of single-member districts, multimember districts, and at-large seats acceptable as remedies in vote-dilution cases?

That depends on whether the plans meet the complete and full remedy standard of section 2. If retaining at-large or multimember seats would perpetuate rather than remedy the voting-rights violation, they cannot be used.

Are single-member districts always the best alternative to at-large elections?

No. While single-member districts are the most commonly used alternative to at-large elections, they do not always provide an adequate remedy. The minority population may be so dispersed that it is impossible to construct districts in which the minority is a majority of the population. Under the circumstances, other election procedures, such as limited or cumulative voting, may provide a more complete and full remedy for the vote dilution.

What are limited and cumulative voting?

In a limited voting system, each voter has fewer votes than the number of seats to be filled. For example, a city council might have five members, but on election day, voters would be instructed to vote for three members or two members or some other number. In a cumulative system, each voter has as many votes as seats to be filled. Voters may give all their votes to one candidate or divide their votes among several candidates. If a minority votes cohesively, both systems enhance its opportunity to elect candidates of its choice and prevent the majority from winning all the seats.

Are practices such as limited and cumulative voting unusual and contrary to American electoral traditions?

No. Limited and cumulative voting have often been used in the United States and have consistently withstood constitutional challenges. While one court has held that they were not required as a remedy for a section 2 violation, they have been voluntarily adopted by the defendants in a number of section 2 cases. They have also been approved by the courts and pre-cleared by the attorney general under section 5 of the Voting Rights Act.

Has the amendment of section 2 had any appreciable impact on voting-rights litigation?

Yes. The amendment of section 2 accelerated the pace of voting-rights litigation. It has brought about a general decline in at-large elections and an increased use of district voting. District voting in turn has facilitated minority political participation and office-holding.

31

Has the amendment of section 2 and the increased use of district voting caused political resegregation and polarization where none existed before?

No. Congress considered such arguments when it amended section 2, and rejected them as unfounded. According to Congress, the evidence presented to it belied the speculations that the amendment of section 2 would be a divisive factor that would polarize communities on the basis of race. Congress concluded that racial polarization was unfortunately already an existing fact of political life. Criticism of the results standard and remedies such as district voting was "like saying that it is the doctor's thermometer which causes high fever."[1]

Social-science studies also show that the increased minority office-holding brought about by district voting has been associated with an increase in responsiveness to minority interests and the inclusion of minorities in decision-making. The presence of minority elected officials has tended to break down polarization and racial stereotyping. It has increased minority access to government.

Are racial minorities *entitled* to elect minority candidates to office in proportion to their presence in the population?

No. The Voting Rights Act provides that no group has a right to have its members elected in numbers equal to its proportion of the population. Thus, a minority could not establish a violation of section 2 merely by showing that there were few minority elected officials. Minorities are, however, entitled to a proportional, or equal, opportunity to elect candidates of their choice.

Are language minorities entitled to special protection in voting?

Yes. The Voting Rights Act requires that a jurisdiction contain-

ing a large language minority (as determined by a special formula) conduct bilingual elections and registration campaigns.
Many states also provide for assistance to illiterate voters or
those who do not read or understand English. Several court
decisions have held that there is a constitutional right to receive
assistance in voting.

Which language minorities are entitled to the special bilingual election and registration provisions of the Voting Rights Act? Which jurisdictions are covered?

The Voting Rights Act defines language minorities as American
Indians, Asian-Americans, Alaskan Natives, and those of Spanish heritage. Jurisdictions required to provide bilingual election procedures for one or more language minorities include
the entire states of Alaska, Arizona, and Texas, and more than
280 counties and townships in California, Colorado, Connecticut, Florida, Hawaii, Idaho, Illinois, Massachusetts, Michigan,
Mississippi, Montana, Nevada, New Jersey, New Mexico, New
York, North Carolina, North Dakota, Oklahoma, Oregon, Penn-
sylvania, Rhode Island, South Dakota, Utah, and Wisconsin.

Are the bilingual registration and election provisions of the act permanent?

No. The bilingual registration and election provisions of the
Voting Rights Act are scheduled to expire on August 6, 2007.

What has been the overall impact of the Voting Rights Act on minority political participation?

It has been substantial. Prior to 1965, there were fewer than 100
black elected officials in the seven southern states originally targeted by the act, and fewer than 200 nationwide. As of January
1993, the number had grown to 3,704 in the targeted states and
8,015 nationwide. Nonblack minorities have posted similar gains.

At the time of passage of the act, there were only about 994,000 black registered voters in the targeted states. By 1992, the number had increased to approximately 4,087,000. Similar increases in black, Hispanic, and Native American registration have been recorded in other parts of the country.

Despite the undeniable progress, minorities clearly have not yet achieved equality of political participation, as measured by office-holding and voter registration and turnout. Nationally, blacks comprise 11 percent of eligible voters but only 1.6 percent of elected offices. The rate of office-holding of other racial minorities is similarly low. Registration and turnout statistics, which are depressed for all voters, also show racial disparities. According to a survey conducted by the Bureau of the Census after the 1992 presidential election, 70 percent of whites but only 64 percent of blacks and 35 percent of Hispanics of voting age were registered to vote, while 64 percent of whites but only 54 percent of blacks and 29 percent of Hispanics of voting age actually voted.

3

EMPLOYMENT

Discrimination in employment is one of the enduring legacies of racial segregation. More individual complaints of employment discrimination are filed each year than perhaps in any other area of civil rights.

Is discrimination in employment on the basis of race prohibited by federal law?

Yes. The most important law prohibiting racial discrimination in employment is Title VII of the Civil Rights Act of 1964.

Which employers are covered by Title VII?

Title VII covers—and hence prohibits discrimination by—all private, state, county, and municipal employers with fifteen or more employees and that are engaged in interstate commerce (the transfer of goods and services between two or more states). The statute prohibits employment discrimination by employment-referral agencies, labor unions with fifteen or more members, and labor apprenticeship programs. Title VII also applies to federal agencies, Congress, and presidential appointments.

What kind of discrimination is prohibited by Title VII?

Title VII makes it unlawful for an employer to discriminate with respect to "compensation, terms, conditions, or privileges of employment" on grounds of race, sex, religion, color, or national origin. The statute prohibits discrimination in hiring, firing, promotion, transfer, job training, and apprenticeship programs. Employment agencies are prohibited from engaging in racial discrimination in referrals for employment. Labor unions may not exclude from membership or segregate any person or make referrals on a discriminatory basis.

What is the standard for determining whether a practice is unlawful under Title VII?

In general, an employment practice is unlawful under Title VII if it constitutes "disparate treatment" of an individual, or has a "disparate impact" upon a group.

How is a violation of the disparate-treatment standard of Title VII shown?

A person must show that he was intentionally treated differently from others because of race. Disparate treatment can be shown by direct evidence, but few employers admit to or have a stated policy of discriminating against minorities. In most cases, disparate treatment must be inferred from the circumstances surrounding an employment decision, such as layoff, promotion, or dismissal.

Employers have broad authority in their employment decisions, and as long as those decisions are not based on race, sex, et cetera, they will stand. Thus, an employer can claim it made the decision based on business conditions or because it simply liked another applicant better. The employer need not prove the absence of a discriminatory motive.

Once the employer gives a non-racial reason for its decision, the minority applicant has the opportunity to show that the stated reason was a pretext. For example, in a 1978 lawsuit against the Jackson, Mississippi, police department, black officers dismissed for allegedly accepting bribes argued that they had been discriminated against. They satisfied their initial burden of proof by showing that white officers accused at the same time of accepting bribes were never even investigated, much less dismissed. The employer then argued that accepting bribes was a legitimate nondiscriminatory reason for dismissal. The court held that in view of the different way in which black and white officers accused of the same conduct were treated, the police department's reason for dismissing the black officers appeared to be a cloak or pretext for discrimination. However, even if a stated reason is a pretext, the complainant does not automatically win. She still has the burden of proving that she was discriminated against on the basis of race.

How is a violation of the disparate-impact standard of Title VII shown?

Disparate-impact cases, unlike disparate-treatment cases, do not require proof of a discriminatory intent. Title VII is aimed at employment practices that have a discriminatory effect, and not simply the motivation of an employer. Because disparate-impact cases focus on the consequences of employment practices, statistics are extremely important and normally provide the evidence of the discrimination.

There are three general steps in proving disparate impact under Title VII. First, a person must show that a practice has a disproportionate impact against racial minorities. Second, the employer must then produce evidence that the practice is related to effective job performance. Third, a challenged practice, even if it is job-related, will still be found unlawful if a complainant can show that some other practice, without a discriminatory effect, would also serve the employer's legitimate interests. Disparate-impact cases, as the example involving the Duke Power Company discussed in the next paragraph shows, require the employer to persuade the court that its practice is job-related or justified by business necessity.

What types of employment practices have been found to have a discriminatory impact, not to be job-related, and therefore unlawful under Title VII?

In a 1971 case, the Duke Power Company in North Carolina had a policy requiring employees seeking promotions either to have a high-school diploma or to make a certain score on an aptitude test. Because of unequal educational opportunities, fewer blacks than whites finished high school and fewer blacks than whites made high scores on the aptitude tests. The company's requirements thus denied promotions to a disproportionate number of minorities. The Supreme Court held that the diploma and test requirements violated Title VII because they had a discriminatory impact, and the company had not shown them to be job-related. Job relatedness might be shown, for example, if high scorers on the test performed better on the job than low scorers. The Supreme Court said that Title VII forbids not only overt discrimination but also practices that are fair in form, but discriminatory in operation. If an employment practice that operates to exclude minorities cannot be shown to be related to job performance, the practice is prohibited.

Can an employer administer ability or other tests in determining whether to hire someone?

Yes. Title VII provides that an employer may use "ability tests" in the hiring process. However, any such test must operate fairly with respect to one race as to another. A test that does not provide the same opportunities to minorities who perform equally well on the job as members of the majority, or that predicts job performance differently because of race, would not be fair and would not be job-related.

Are there any employment practices that have a discriminatory effect and are not job-related that are lawful under Title VII?

Yes. Seniority systems, regardless of their discriminatory impact and regardless of whether they are job-related, are lawful under Title VII—unless they were formulated with an intent to discriminate. A discriminatory intent cannot be inferred, but must be proved by facts showing actual motive. It is very difficult to prove that a seniority system violates Title VII.

Are there any other exceptions to the nondiscrimination provisions of Title VII?

Yes. An employer may discriminate on the basis of sex, religion, or national origin in very limited circumstances where the characteristics are a "bona fide occupational qualification" (BFOQ). That means the discrimination is necessary to the normal operation of the employer's business or activity. For example, a college supported by a particular religious denomination might refuse to hire as a teacher a person who was not a member of that denomination. There is no BFOQ exception that allows employment decisions to be based on race.

Can there be a violation of Title VII where discrimination was only one of several factors in an employer's decision?

Yes. Intentional discrimination in employment is always unlawful. A person who has been discriminated against is entitled to a court order ending the discrimination and attorneys' fees. He cannot recover any monetary damages, however, if the employer shows that it would have made the same decision for reasons that had nothing to do with discrimination. Thus, a person dismissed because he was frequently late for work *and* because he was black or Hispanic could not recover back pay or money damages for pain and suffering.

What is a racially hostile workforce? Is it prohibited by Title VII?

A racially hostile workforce is one which is permeated with racial intimidation, ridicule, and insult. Title VII prohibits an employer from creating or permitting others to create such a working environment.

How does one prove that a workforce is hostile?

An employee must show that the racial hostility was severe enough to create an abusive working environment. She is not required to show that she was actually injured emotionally or psychologically.

Does Title VII apply to Americans working for United States companies abroad?

Yes. However, the actions of a company otherwise prohibited by Title VII are exempt from coverage to the extent that they would violate the law of the foreign country in which the company's workplace is located. For example, an American company abroad would not violate Title VII by complying with a foreign country's restrictions on the employment of women or a racial group.

Are there other federal laws that prohibit racial discrimination in employment?

Yes. The Thirteenth Amendment and part of the Civil Rights Act of 1866 (42 U.S.C. § 1981) prohibit discrimination in making and enforcing contracts for public and private employment. (Section 1981 has been held to apply to discrimination against Jews and Arabs, as well as African-Americans.) The Fourteenth Amendment and part of the Civil Rights Act of 1871 (42 U.S.C. § 1983) prohibit discrimination in state and local government employment.

Presidential executive orders require all federal contracts to include an "equal opportunity clause." By signing a contract, a private contractor agrees not to discriminate in hiring and to take affirmative action to eliminate discrimination. Firms with at least 50 employees that contract with the government for fifty thousand dollars or more must also file affirmative-action plans setting forth steps for achieving equal employment.

Are there important differences between Title VII and the older Reconstruction-era prohibitions against employment discrimination?

Yes. There are three important differences. First, although Title VII and the older federal prohibitions sometimes cover the same employers, very often they do not. The Thirteenth Amendment and § 1981 prohibit all private employers, and unions too, whatever their size, from engaging in intentional discrimination. It is also irrelevant whether an employer is

41

engaged in interstate commerce. Second, Title VII is administered by a federal agency, the Equal Employment Opportunity
Commission (EEOC). It has the duty of investigating and trying
to resolve claims of discrimination before they are taken to
court. Third, Title VII prohibits a larger variety of practices
than do the older federal prohibitions. The older laws prohibit
only intentionally discriminatory practices. Title VII prohibits
intentionally discriminatory practices as well as those that
have a discriminatory effect.

How does one prove that an employment practice is intentionally discriminatory under the Constitution or the Reconstruction-era statutes?

First, it is not necessary to prove that an action is motivated
solely by a racially discriminatory purpose, but only that a
discriminatory purpose was a factor. Second, determining
whether a discriminatory purpose was a factor requires a court
to look at whatever direct or circumstantial evidence of intent
may be available. A starting point is the racial impact of the
practice. The historical background of the decision is another
source of evidence. Departures from the normal procedural
sequence also might be evidence that an improper purpose
played a role. For example, if a company never required written recommendations from white job applicants but implemented such a requirement only when a black applied for
employment, the departure from the company's normal procedure could be considered as evidence of discrimination.

Do the states have laws prohibiting discrimination in employment?

Yes, most states do. Many counties and cities also have enacted laws making certain forms of employment discrimination
unlawful.

REMEDIES FOR EMPLOYMENT DISCRIMINATION

What remedies are available to persons who have been discriminated against in employment in violation of Title VII?

One of the purposes of Title VII is to make persons whole for injuries suffered on account of unlawful employment discrimination—that is, to restore them to the condition or status they would have been in had the discrimination not occurred. Applying this standard, the courts have ordered as remedies for Title VII violations: (1) termination of the discrimination; (2) hiring, reinstatement, or promotion; (3) awards of back pay and retroactive seniority; and sometimes, (4) affirmative measures such as goals for hiring minorities and timetables for accomplishing the hiring. Hiring goals and timetables are discussed in more detail later in this chapter and in the chapter on race-conscious remedies. Court-awarded attorneys' fees, including the cost of hiring expert witnesses, are available for the prevailing party in a Title VII lawsuit.

How much back pay is available to a person who has been discriminated against in violation of Title VII?

Pursuant to the make-whole objective of Title VII, an award of back pay is determined by the amount of pay that normally would have been earned if there had been no discrimination. Back pay awards may also include interest, overtime, vacation, and sick pay, as well as pension-plan contributions. There are, however, two important limitations.

First, back pay is calculated no further back than two years prior to the date upon which an administrative charge of discrimination was filed with the EEOC. Thus, for example, even if a person had been discriminatorily denied a promotion for ten years, she would be eligible under Title VII to receive back pay only starting two years before filing a charge of discrimination with the EEOC.

Second, the amount of back pay for which a person is eligible is reduced by the amount a person earned or could have earned. For example, if a person earned $400 a week at the time he was fired and immediately found a new job making $300 a week, he would normally be able to recover $100 a week back pay.

Are monetary damages, other than back pay, available under Title VII for unlawful employment discrimination?

Yes, but only to those (for example, women), who cannot recover damages under § 1981. Congress placed a ceiling, or cap, on the amount of damages that can be recovered based on the size of the employer's workforce. Back pay is excluded from the cap. The cap applies to each complaining party rather than an entire group of employees affected by a discriminatory policy or practice. Thus, if a company discriminated against several employees, their damages for purposes of the cap would be computed individually rather than collectively.

Under Title VII, is retroactive seniority an available remedy for unlawful employment discrimination?

Yes. Persons who have been discriminated against are entitled to the seniority they would have earned had they not been discriminated against. Even though a seniority system may itself be lawful, a person who has been unlawfully discriminated against is entitled to full retroactive seniority.

Are remedies similar to those available under Title VII also available in lawsuits filed under the older Reconstruction amendments and civil-rights acts?

Yes. Once a person has proved intentional discrimination under the older laws, similar remedies are available.

Are monetary damages, other than back pay, available under the older civil-rights prohibitions?

Yes. Persons discriminated against may receive not only back pay, but other out-of-pocket expenses and possible pain and suffering damages. If the discrimination is found to have been malicious, a court can award punitive damages. Punitive damages are designed to punish a wrongdoer and prevent a recurrence of the unlawful acts. Punitive damages are very difficult to obtain because it is very hard to prove malicious discrimination.

Are other remedies, such as affirmative hiring of minorities and goals and timetables for accomplishing the hiring, available under Title VII or the Constitution to make up for extensive past discrimination?

Yes. In most employment cases, a court need only require an employer to stop practicing the discrimination and award make-whole relief to the individual victims of the discrimination. But in some instances where discrimination has been persistent, it may be necessary to require an employer to take affirmative steps to end the discrimination. A court might require an employer—public or private—to hire qualified minorities roughly in proportion to the number of qualified minorities in the workforce.

In a 1989 case involving the city of Buffalo, New York, after finding that the city had discriminated in employment in its police and fire departments, the court required the city to make 50 percent of its appointments from a pool of qualified minority applicants. The hiring goals were to remain in effect until the city's workforce reflected the minority composition of the labor force.

How does a court determine whether affirmative-action remedies are necessary in a particular case?

The court looks at a variety of factors, including: the extent of the past discrimination; the availability and effectiveness of alternative remedies; the flexibility, duration, and waivability of the relief, that is, whether the time for complying with the goals is reasonable and whether failure to achieve the goals could be excused for a good reason; the impact of the relief on third parties, such as nonminority job applicants, who themselves may be innocent of any discrimination; and the relationship of the numerical goals to the relevant labor market, for example, whether there is a sufficient number of minority job applicants in the area from which the employer hires to meet the hiring goals.

Applying these standards, the Supreme Court approved a remedy requiring Alabama, which had systematically excluded blacks from employment in its Department of Public Safety, to promote one black trooper for each white trooper promoted, as long as qualified black candidates were available, until the imbalance was corrected. The Court found the affirmative-action remedy permissible because it was flexible, waivable, temporary in application, and did not impose an unacceptable burden on innocent third parties.

Can a court award seniority retroactively to a class, or group of employees, as part of a general affirmative-action remedy?

No. A court can award seniority only where the beneficiary of the award has actually been a victim of illegal discrimination.

Can a state or local government voluntarily adopt an affirmative-action plan?

Yes, but such plans—because they contain classifications based on race—are subject to strict scrutiny. That means they are constitutionally suspect and may be used only if they promote a compelling governmental interest and are narrowly tai-

lored to further that interest. Examples of compelling governmental interests would be remedying or avoiding a violation of
federal law or in overcoming the effects of past discrimination.
A remedy would be narrowly tailored if, as in the Alabama
troopers case, it was flexible, waivable, and temporary, and did
not treat innocent parties unfairly.

Are voluntary affirmative-action plans by private employers designed to integrate the workforce and forestall possible employment-discrimination litigation permissible under Title VII?

Yes, depending on the facts and circumstances involved. In a
1979 case, involving steelworkers at Kaiser Aluminum &
Chemical Corporation's plant in Gramercy, Louisiana, the
union and the company entered into a voluntary affirmative-
action agreement to eliminate racial imbalance in the company's almost exclusively white workforce. Under the agreement,
the company set a goal of 39 percent minority representation
(the minority representation in the surrounding labor force),
adopted a hiring ratio of one minority for every white (so that
50 percent of the new skilled employees would be minority
workers), and estimated that its goal would be reached within
30 years. A white employee brought suit, claiming that the
agreement was reverse discrimination, but the Supreme Court
rejected the challenge.

The Court acknowledged that Title VII protected whites as
well as blacks from racial discrimination in employment, but
concluded that the statute did not forbid all voluntary race-
conscious affirmative action. In the Court's view, the spirit and
intent of Title VII was to break down old patterns of racial segregation, and to open job opportunities for minority workers.
The Court then found that the specific plan adopted by the
company was permissible in that it did not require the dis-

charge of white workers, nor was it a bar to their advancement. The plan was a temporary measure to eliminate an obvious racial imbalance, not to maintain racial balance.

Are voluntary affirmative-action plans that give preferential protection against layoffs to minority employees lawful under Title VII?

No. The Court invalidated an affirmative-action agreement under which a school board gave preferences to minority employees in layoffs. When it became necessary to reduce the workforce, nonminority teachers were laid off while minority teachers with less seniority were retained. The nonminority teachers brought suit, and the Supreme Court held that the layoffs treated the more experienced teachers unfairly by making them shoulder the entire burden of achieving racial fairness in hiring. The school board's affirmative-action plan was too intrusive and was not sufficiently narrowly tailored to accomplish its purposes.

Some cities and states adopt programs that set aside a certain percentage of funds to be used in contracts with minority firms, in order to increase minority employment opportunities. Are these programs lawful under the Constitution?

Yes, but they are also subject to strict scrutiny. Failing to meet this test was a "set-aside" program adopted by the city of Richmond requiring contractors with whom the city did business to subcontract at least 30 percent of the dollar amount of the contract to one or more minority businesses. The Court found that the city failed to produce any evidence that nonminority contractors had systematically excluded minority businesses from subcontracting opportunities. The city also failed to show that there was a significant statistical disparity between the number of qualified minority contractors willing and able to perform a particular service and the number of such contractors actually employed. Because the city failed to identify the need for remedial action, its set-aside program violated the Fourteenth Amendment. The Court indicated that such a plan would be constitutional if good reasons were offered to support it. Indeed, since the Richmond decision in 1989, a number of local set-asides have been approved by the lower federal courts.

Are set-asides authorized by Congress judged by the same standards as those adopted by cities and states?

Yes. Although the courts normally grant special deference to Congress as a co-equal branch of government, federal set-asides are judged by the same strict standards as those for cities and counties.

Does affirmative action violate the make-whole rationale of Title VII by benefiting those who are not themselves victims of discrimination?

No. The Supreme Court has held that the purpose of affirmative-action remedies is not to make identified victims whole but to dismantle prior patterns of employment discrimination and to prevent discrimination in the future. Relief is provided to the class as a whole rather than to individual members.

Does affirmative action treat people unfairly who are themselves innocent of discrimination by denying them employment and other opportunities?

That depends on how heavy and intrusive the burdens of affirmative action are. The courts are concerned about possible injury to third parties when affirmative-action plans are adopted, and for that reason, as noted above, the Supreme Court invalidated a provision in an agreement that laid off white teachers with more seniority than recently hired minorities. However, because of the nation's dedication to eradicating racial discrimination, even innocent third parties may be called upon to bear some of the burdens of affirmative action, provided those burdens are diffuse and not overly intrusive.

Can those who were not parties to a discrimination lawsuit challenge a decision implementing affirmative action on the grounds that it harms them?

Nonminorities have been allowed to challenge affirmative-action plans on the ground that they denied nonminorities opportunities for employment and promotion. However, such challenges are not permitted if the nonminority had notice of the lawsuit and a reasonable opportunity to intervene but failed to act. In addition, a later challenge would not be permitted if the court had already rejected a similar claim. The rules limiting intervention are designed to achieve finality and fairness in employment discrimination cases—cases which include hiring or promotion orders that might affect the rights of nonminorities.

PROCEDURES UNDER TITLE VII OF THE CIVIL RIGHTS ACT OF 1964

In order to be protected by Title VII in nonfederal employment, are there any procedural steps which must be taken?

Yes. The procedural steps are very important and must be strictly adhered to. A claim must be filed with the EEOC within 180 days of the discriminatory act. If the state or locality has an agency similar to the EEOC that can enforce a state or local law prohibiting discrimination in employment, a claim must also be filed with that agency within the time limit specified by the local law.

The generally accepted view is that a complainant's Title VII action is not barred by failing to file a charge within a state limitations period if the state period is shorter than the 180-day period under the federal statute. The EEOC will not, however, investigate a Title VII charge until the state or local agency has had 60 days to review the charge, or if an investigation has begun within 60 days.

Where and how do you file a charge of discrimination under Title VII?

A person may file an administrative charge of discrimination with any district or regional office of the EEOC, or with the main office of the EEOC in Washington, D.C. The EEOC has an official form for filing administrative charges.

What does the EEOC do after it receives a charge of discrimination?

Within ten days after receiving a charge, the EEOC must notify the employer of the allegation of discrimination. The EEOC is then supposed to investigate the charge to determine if there is reasonable cause to believe a violation of Title VII has occurred; or the EEOC will refer the charge to the appropriate state or local agency, if one exists, for 60 days. The investigation by the EEOC is supposed to last no longer than 120 days after the filing of the charge or after the 60-day local or state agency deferral period.

If the EEOC finds reasonable cause, it will try to convince both sides to settle the matter. If it fails, the EEOC can file a lawsuit in federal district court against the employer for an order ending the discrimination and other relief.

Is there much chance that the EEOC will resolve the charge of discrimination?

No. The EEOC has a large backlog of charges of discrimination. It has been unable to resolve many claims.

If the EEOC does not resolve a charge of discrimination, can a complainant go to court under Title VII to remedy the discrimination?

Yes. A complainant may sue in court after 180 days have elapsed since the filing of the charge and after receiving a "right-to-sue letter" from the EEOC (to sue private employers) or from the Justice Department (to sue state, county, and municipal employers). Alternatively, if the EEOC certifies that it will not investigate the charge within 180 days, an individual may ask for a right-to-sue letter and bring suit immediately. However, the individual *must* sue, if at all, within 90 days after receiving the right-to-sue letter.

Can a person who can't afford a lawyer still file a lawsuit under Title VII?

Yes. Under Title VII, a low-income person can file a lawsuit *in forma pauperis*, which means that she or he can sue without paying court costs. And one can always file a lawsuit *pro se*, which means that a person can represent himself. But since the law is very complicated, it is best to try to find a lawyer.

If a person who has been discriminated against cannot file a lawsuit under Title VII, are there other possible means of obtaining relief from a court?

Yes. First, the EEOC can sue private employers and unions. The Justice Department can sue state, county, and municipal employers. Although they file very few lawsuits, it is sometimes worth contacting them to see if they will sue. Second, a person can sue under the Thirteenth and Fourteenth Amendments and the older Reconstruction-era statutes without complying with any of the procedural requirements of Title VII. However, the complaint must be filed within the period set by state law for bringing a lawsuit (known as the statute of limitations).

How does a person file a charge of discrimination against an employer that has contracts with the federal government?

Employees who work for companies that have contracts with the federal government and that are prohibited from discriminating by executive order may file charges of discrimination with the Office of Federal Contract Compliance Programs (OFCCP) of the Department of Labor within 180 days of the violation. Although the OFCCP has responsibility for the administration and enforcement of the executive order, it transfers individual complaints of employment discrimination to the EEOC for investigation and processing under Title VII.

How about discrimination in federal agencies? Are the Title VII procedures the same?

No. Persons seeking the protection of Title VII against federal agencies—other than Congress, the agencies of the legislative branch, and presidential appointments—are governed by a separate set of complicated procedures that are even more difficult to follow than those applicable to discrimination by nonfederal employers. Furthermore, the initial steps must be undertaken not with the EEOC but instead with the federal agency itself.

Briefly, a complaint must be filed with the agency's Equal Employment Opportunity Counselor (within 90 days of the discriminatory act) and with the agency itself. The agency is given an opportunity to investigate the complaint and attempt to resolve it. If it fails, the employee can appeal to the EEOC and/or file a lawsuit. The time periods within which an employee is required to act are very short, but must be complied with to get the protection offered by Title VII.

Is there a good chance that the responsible federal agency will resolve the charge of discrimination?

No. Most federal agencies have reputations for being unable to resolve their own discrimination.

How are employment-discrimination complaints against Congress, the agencies of the legislative branch, and in presidential appointments processed under Title VII?

In the Senate, complaints of discrimination in employment are investigated by the Office of Senate Fair Employment Practices, pursuant to a special set of rules enacted by Congress. Upon completion of the administrative process, an appeal may be taken to the United States Court of Appeals for the District of Columbia.

In the House of Representatives, employment-discrimination claims are investigated by a review board, under procedures established by the House. The chief official of each agency of the legislative branch is required to adopt rules to be used in processing complaints.

Complaints by presidential appointees against the president or other appointing authority in the executive branch are processed by the EEOC. An appeal may be taken to the United States Court of Appeals for the District of Columbia.

Can an employer fire or retaliate against an employee for filing an EEOC complaint or speaking out against discrimination on the job?

No. Title VII makes it illegal for an employer to retaliate in any way against a person who files a charge of discrimination or cooperates with the EEOC. Title VII has also been interpreted to prohibit the discharge of an employee for lawful civil-rights activities whether or not they involve the EEOC.

Not all forms of protest against discrimination are protected by Title VII. The courts have balanced the goal of fair-employment laws with the right of employers to select and supervise their employees. An employee who filed a charge of discrimination with the EEOC, for example, was not protected from discharge where the employer showed that the employee had a long history of absenteeism and that other employees with similar records had also been discharged.

In determining if an employer's actions are prohibited by Title VII, some courts have asked whether the employee's protest was calculated to inflict needless economic hardship on the employer. For example, in 1976, a federal court held that a research foundation in Massachusetts could fire an employee whose complaint went beyond legitimate accusations of discrimination and who disclosed confidential information to newspaper reporters and circulated rumors that the foundation was in financial trouble. An employee was protected from retaliation, however, for writing and circulating a petition protesting racial discrimination and urging other employees to assert their legal rights. The courts have also protected complaining employees who had a reasonable belief that a practice was discriminatory, even if the charge was later found to be without merit.

4

EDUCATION

For many, the modern civil-rights era began with the United
States Supreme Court's historic, unanimous decision in *Brown
v. Board of Education*.[1] "Separate educational facilities," the
Supreme Court declared, "are inherently unequal." Within several years, the Supreme Court had applied this decision widely
to end segregation in numerous government facilities and services. Segregation in public education, however, did not end
with the Supreme Court's 1954 decision. In fact, the Supreme
Court did not even create a remedy for unconstitutional segregation until the following year. Even then, the Court only
directed the school boards that had been sued to desegregate
their school systems with "all deliberate speed."

Unfortunately, for the next 20 years, most school districts
around the country focused on the term "deliberate" and not
the word "speed," using many different strategies to resist
desegregation. Despite this resistance to desegregation, the
Supreme Court established the right of racial minorities to be
free of legally enforced school segregation. In recent years,

this principle has been expanded to include the right to be free of school segregation (racial separation) caused by the practices of nearby school districts (for example, state officials contributing to racial segregation by manipulating school-district lines, or by discriminatory use of housing laws), the right to a bilingual education for students with limited English proficiency, and the right to nondiscriminatory admissions procedures in private schools. These rights, however, are usually enforceable only through lawsuits filed by people who believe their rights have been violated by a school board.

PUBLIC-SCHOOL SEGREGATION

Is a school that is almost all of one race unconstitutional?

It depends. Federal courts will declare a racially imbalanced school unconstitutional only if the segregation resulted from intentional acts of discrimination. The state courts have not yet addressed this question fully. Although school districts have the power to require that schools have a racial ratio reflecting the proportion for the district as a whole, the courts impose no general requirement of racial balance. Only where school districts have intentionally engaged in segregation in violation of the Equal Protection Clause of the Fourteenth Amendment are racial balance and student reassignment on the basis of race legally required.

What forms of school segregation violate the Fourteenth Amendment's guarantee of equal protection of the laws?

In *Brown*, the Supreme Court declared intentional, state-imposed, racially segregated school systems to be a violation of the Fourteenth Amendment. Also, any state-enforced dual school system that requires black students to attend separate, all-black schools violates the Fourteenth Amendment.

What do courts do to address an unconstitutional state-imposed dual school system?

The Supreme Court requires segregated school systems to make a transition to racially nondiscriminatory systems and to eliminate all aspects of dual education systems until state-imposed segregation has been completely removed. If school districts do not cooperate, they can be forced to desegregate through lawsuits. If a federal court determines that a school district or a state has failed to carry out its duty to desegregate, it may order appropriate remedies (solutions).

The Supreme Court has adopted the following as remedies for school segregation: reassign teachers and students according to mathematical ratios based upon race; alter attendance zones (district lines used to determine the location of one's school) and feeder patterns (plans used to place children in particular schools); realign bus transportation routes; provide services such as special reading programs; and provide in-service human-relations training for teachers.

Does school segregation in the North and West, which state law did not impose, also violate the Fourteenth Amendment?

Generally speaking, the answer is yes. *Intentional* policies and practices of school authorities caused most of the segregation in the North and West. These policies and practices violate the Fourteenth Amendment as much as segregation imposed by state laws in the South. In other words, even when not mandated by law, segregation violates the U.S. Constitution when it results from deliberate government action.

The Supreme Court has outlined some of the policies and

practices that create a segregated school system and consequently violate the Fourteenth Amendment: drawing attendance zones or creating feeder schools on the basis of race to concentrate blacks in certain schools; building schools of a certain size and in a specific location fully aware that those schools would be segregated; and using mobile classrooms, drafting student transfer policies, transporting students, and assigning faculty and staff on racially identifiable bases.

Does the claim by a school district that it has not intentionally discriminated and that it has only followed a neighborhood assignment policy mean the school district has no responsibility for the segregation of its schools?

No. School districts frequently argue that the existence of any school segregation merely results from residential segregation. The courts will closely examine such claims. A close review of neighborhood assignment policies often reveals that students are not, in fact, assigned to the nearest school. Instead these school officials assign children based on race, and establish school assignment and feeder patterns to parallel racial residential changes. Federal courts have recognized this interrelationship between housing and school segregation. For example, one federal court found both the city and the school board responsible for school segregation. The city created segregated housing by locating most public housing in communities of color; the school board, for its part, used its neighborhood school policy to increase school segregation further.

If school officials intentionally segregate only a portion of a school system, will the courts require the entire system to desegregate to correct racial imbalance?

Yes, if the discrimination has been significant and has had a system-wide impact. The Supreme Court has determined that the existence of a school board's intentional segregation in part of a school system creates a presumption that any segregation in the school system is intentional. When a system-wide effect occurs—in other words, the whole school system is segregated—the entire system must desegregate. However, if only a very small portion of a school system is unconstitutionally segregated, and the segregation has no significant impact on the system as a whole, desegregating the entire school district is not mandatory.

Are the remedies for segregation caused by school officials carrying out intentionally discriminatory policies and practices the same as those for segregation caused by state laws?

Yes.

When a school district is unconstitutionally segregated and a court-ordered desegregation plan is imposed, will the plan stay in effect for many years? Can the plan be altered to correct increasing racial imbalance in the school district?

Once a court imposes a desegregation plan, the plan usually will stay in effect for several years to ensure the removal of all remaining effects of segregation from the school district. Several federal courts have indicated that districts must follow the requirements of the desegregation plan for at least three years in a row.

Courts have used different standards, however, when determining whether a school system has successfully desegregated or, in other words, changed from a dual to a unitary system. The Supreme Court has stated that a "dual" system exists when a school system has engaged in intentional racial segregation of students, in effect creating two school systems.

"Unitary" status exists when a school system is one integrated system, and when all students have equal access to educational resources and opportunities.

The Supreme Court has also declared that federal supervision of local school systems should be temporary. The Court set out the standard for lower courts when considering whether a desegregation plan can be dissolved. First, the school district must genuinely try to comply with the court order. Second, the school district must eliminate, as much as possible, all remnants of segregation in its faculty, staff, transportation, extracurricular activities, and facilities. A court order to desegregate, however, does not mean that every school must reflect the racial composition of the entire community. Mathematical ratios provide only a starting point for shaping a remedy; they do not establish a fixed requirement.

The Supreme Court has established three criteria for courts to use to determine if a district has achieved unitary status: (1) whether the district complied with the desegregation plan, (2) whether continuing court control is necessary to achieve compliance, and (3) whether the district genuinely tried to desegregate. The Court has also ruled that a school district under a desegregation order can achieve desegregated or unitary status over a period of time. For example, one year the district can become unitary in student assignments and the following year in teacher placement.

In view of the flight of whites from desegregated schools, are desegregation remedies useless when applied to central-city schools?

No. First, even in predominantly minority school districts, many whites do remain after desegregation. There is no difference, in principle, between desegregating a school district with 70 percent minority and 30 percent white students, and desegregating one with the reverse proportions. The objective in both situations is to eliminate the effects of intentional racial segregation caused by school authorities.

Second, white flight is not a recent phenomenon due solely to school desegregation. This phenomenon began with suburbanization after World War II and has continued up to the present. In fact, much of the suburbanization of whites and the concentration of minorities in central cities has been caused by government action. Regardless of whether white flight has occurred, the current situation in many metropolitan schools has been caused by government policies and actions such as discriminatory zoning laws or government-supported mortgage lending that has a discriminatory effect. Under these circumstances, courts may impose desegregation plans that include city as well as suburban school districts.

Does interdistrict segregation violate the Fourteenth Amendment when a central city school district is predominantly minority and suburban districts are predominantly white?

Interdistrict segregation occurs when neighboring districts become racially segregated. Typically, this usually appears as suburban districts that are predominantly white surrounding a central-city district that is predominantly students of color. Interdistrict segregation violates the Fourteenth Amendment only if the suburban districts as well as the central city district have broken the law in a way that has effects beyond their respective district boundaries (for example, if city district authorities transfer white students to suburban districts, or if government officials, such as the governor or members of the state legislature, otherwise contribute to the segregation of neighborhoods).

In *Milliken v. Bradley*,[2] the Supreme Court ruled that a desegregation plan that involved both the city of Detroit and the Detroit-area suburban schools was improper. The Court said that an interdistrict desegregation plan might be appropriate if it is shown that a constitutional violation in one district produces significant segregation in another district. The Court also stated that an interdistrict desegregation plan might be proper if state officials had contributed to racial segregation by manipulating school-district lines, or by discriminatory use of state housing or zoning laws.

Although a Supreme Court ruling in 1995 considered an expanded definition of interdistrict remedies which included the creation of a magnet school system within Kansas City, it declared such a remedy to be unjustified by the existence of white flight. (Magnet schools are public schools that offer distinctive curriculum designed to draw students from different neighborhoods.) In *Missouri v. Jenkins*,[3] the Court found no interdistrict violation that would justify an interdistrict remedy, because it believed that the central city's desegregation policies *alone* induced white flight. The Court considered but then rejected imposing a magnet school system.

Within the last ten years, state courts have begun to address interdistrict segregation under state constitutional provisions. Many state constitutions include a clause guaranteeing students' rights to an adequate education. Recent attacks on school-segregation suits have utilized these state provisions. In 1996, the Connecticut Supreme Court ruled that racial segregation in the Hartford schools violated the Connecticut Constitution. Unlike federal requirements, the Connecticut Supreme Court did not require evidence of intentional discrimination by the state, only the existence of segregation.

Have any interdistrict school desegregation lawsuits been successful after the Supreme Court's decision in the Detroit case of *Milliken*?

Yes. As a result of two successful lawsuits, interdistrict desegregation plans have been implemented in metropolitan Louisville, Kentucky, and in metropolitan Wilmington, Delaware. Both lawsuits produced an interdistrict desegregation plan because of violations of the Equal Protection Clause of the U.S. Constitution. The Supreme Court did not review either case.

In Louisville, the existence of interdistrict school segregation whereby the city and suburbs had assigned minority students to all-black schools in the city provided the primary basis of the interdistrict remedy. In Wilmington, the court approved an interdistrict school remedy to address unconstitutional government contributions to segregated residential patterns. Nearly all low-cost public housing in the metropolitan area had been placed in Wilmington. In addition, government officials had accepted deeds containing racially restrictive covenants (agreements which restricted the use of property based on race). Moreover, the State Real Estate Commission Handbook had encouraged single-race neighborhoods, as had the Federal Mortgage Underwriting Manual.

If minority students believe that they are unconstitutionally segregated, how can they enforce their rights?

A lawsuit filed by students and their parents or guardians under the Fourteenth Amendment of the U.S. Constitution, under part of the Civil Rights Act of 1871, or under the adequate-education or equal-protection clauses of a state constitution, provides the primary means for individuals to eliminate discrimination in public education. Remedies come in the form of court-ordered desegregation, as discussed above. Monetary damages have rarely, if ever, been recovered.

Aside from lawsuits brought by individuals, are there any other ways to remedy discrimination in public schools?

Yes. First, two civil-rights laws authorize the Department of Justice (DOJ) to file discrimination lawsuits against school districts. Under one section of Title IV of the Civil Rights Act of 1964, the DOJ may file a lawsuit if it receives a written charge from parents alleging discrimination and if the DOJ certifies that the parents cannot bring a lawsuit on their own behalf. Similarly, under several sections of the Equal Education Opportunities Act of 1974, the DOJ may file a lawsuit on behalf of any "individual denied an equal educational opportunity." Although the DOJ files very few such lawsuits, it is worth sending an administrative charge of discrimination to the Department of Justice in Washington, D.C.

A second possibility involves desegregation enforcement by the Department of Education (DOE). Title VI of the Civil Rights Act of 1964 requires the DOE to terminate its federal funding to discriminatory school districts. Because of its importance, this remedy will be discussed in detail in chapter 7.

SCHOOL FINANCING AND BILINGUAL EDUCATION

Do racial minorities enjoy other educational rights?

Yes and no. Although enforcement of the right to a desegregated education has exposed many educational inequities besides segregation, these have not been uniformly addressed. Three important areas of educational inequity other than segregation include disparities in school financing, the absence of bilingual education, and the absence of a minimally adequate educational standard.

The Supreme Court has ruled that there is no enforceable right under the Fourteenth Amendment to equitable school financing. A growing number of state courts, however, have declared that such a right exists. The federal courts have established a right to a bilingual education for racial minorities with limited English proficiency. Finally, state courts have begun to address minimally adequate education under state constitutions.

What inequities exist in school financing?

Public-school districts generally receive support from a combination of sources: (1) state funds awarded fairly equally to each district, based upon the number of students attending schools in the district, and (2) local property taxes. Local property taxes not only provide the greatest monetary support for school districts, but also remain highly unequal. For example, a low-income, predominantly minority urban school district may tax its residents heavily but raise relatively little revenue for its schools. In contrast, an affluent, predominantly suburban school district (which are usually predominantly white) may tax its residents only slightly but still raise much greater revenues for its schools. These inequities in school financing prove particularly harsh to low-income racial minorities because of the high taxation imposed on them and the low revenues raised for their schools.

If school financing inequities are so obvious, why are they not unconstitutional under the Fourteenth Amendment?

In 1972, the Supreme Court declared that school financing inequities do not violate the Fourteenth Amendment's guarantee of equal protection of the laws because education is not a fundamental right under the U.S. Constitution. Wide disparities could exist in education so long as such practices do not appear unreasonable. The Court focused on this country's long tradition of local control over schools, adding that "some inequality" did not provide a sufficient basis for striking down a financing system. The Court did note, however, that if children attending school in the poorly financed area had been denied an education altogether, a Fourteenth Amendment claim might exist.

Several state courts have approached education issues differently and found a fundamental right to an adequate education under their state constitutions.

How do courts interpret a "minimally adequate education"?

In minimum-standard cases, courts hold states responsible for failing to ensure an adequate education, defined as the failure of a state's students to attain the minimum standards. What constitutes a minimally adequate education may vary from state to state and depends on the laws that set up programs and/or requirements intended to improve the educational performance of students. In the Massachusetts case *McDuffy v. Secretary of Education* (1993), the court articulated a seven-prong definition of educational adequacy: (1) oral and written communication skills sufficient to function in a complex and rapidly changing world; (2) knowledge of economic, social, and political systems sufficient to make informed choices; (3) understanding of governmental processes sufficient to understand local and national issues; (4) self-knowledge and knowledge of mental and physical wellness; (5) grounding in the arts sufficient to appreciate culture; (6) preparation in vocational or academic fields sufficient to choose and pursue work intelligently; and (7) academic or vocational skills sufficient to compete favorably in academics or job markets.

Can school financing inequities be challenged other than through a lawsuit filed under the Fourteenth Amendment?

Yes. A number of school financing challenges have been brought in state courts alleging discrimination in violation of the equal-protection clauses of state constitutions. Because the Supreme Court cannot review interpretations of state constitutions, state courts can differ from the Supreme Court's interpretation of the Fourteenth Amendment in regard to educational inequities.

In the early 1970s, California (1971), Connecticut (1974), and New Jersey (1973) interpreted their state constitutions to prohibit property-tax school-financing inequalities. More recently, four state courts—in Arkansas, California, Connecticut, and Wyoming—have found that school district disparities violated their state's equal-protection clause. In addition, every state but Mississippi has an education clause in their state constitution guaranteeing free public education to its citizens. Several states—Kentucky, Montana, New Jersey, Texas, Washington, and West Virginia—have found funding disparities in violation of this clause.

What is a bilingual education?

Bilingual education generally means the effective education of students with limited English proficiency who come from environments where the dominant language is other than English. In order to provide an effective bilingual education, schools teach the students English, but they teach all other subjects in the students' dominant language until the students can learn other subjects in English.

Congress recently heralded bilingual education as an educational priority. When enacting the Bilingual Education Act, it acknowledged "the special educational needs of the large numbers of children of limited English speaking ability in the United States" and declared "it to be the policy of the United States to provide financial assistance to local educational agencies to develop and carry out" bilingual educational programs.

Do students with limited English proficiency have a right to a bilingual education?

Yes. The Supreme Court ruled that such a right exists, at least when there are a substantial number of non- or limited-English-speaking students who speak the same dominant language.

How do students with limited English proficiency enforce their right to a bilingual education?

The primary method is to file a lawsuit against the school district alleging a violation of Title VI of the Civil Rights Act of 1964. Before such a lawsuit can be filed, an administrative charge of discrimination must be filed with the federal agency, the Department of Education (DOE), that administers Title VI regarding schools. The charge may be resolved administratively by DOE without having to file a lawsuit. Complaints should be sent to any DOE regional office or the main office.

DISCRIMINATION IN PRIVATE SCHOOLS

Are there any prohibitions against discrimination in private, as opposed to public, schools?

Yes. As we have seen, the Fourteenth Amendment's guarantee of equal protection of the laws prohibits discrimination in public education. The Fourteenth Amendment, however, applies only to state and local governments, not to private entities.

But this does not mean that discrimination is permitted in private schools. Two federal laws prohibit private-school discrimination: (1) the Civil Rights Act of 1866, which protects minority contract rights (the right to enter into an agreement between two or more persons which creates an obligation to do or not to do a particular thing) and (2) Title VI of the Civil Rights Act of 1964, which prohibits discrimination in programs or activities receiving federal financial assistance. Administrative procedures and lawsuits, both of which will be discussed in chapter 7, provide the primary means to enforce Title VI.

AFFIRMATIVE ACTION IN ADMISSIONS

What does affirmative action mean in educational admissions?

Affirmative action in admissions embodies two closely related concepts. First, affirmative action requires special recruitment of racial minorities. This enables predominantly white colleges and universities, which may have used or may still use admissions criteria that discriminate against minority applicants (for example, many institutions evaluate applicants by criteria clearly unrelated to a student's ability to perform, such as her parents' wealth and whether her parents were alumni; these criteria have a discriminatory effect on minority applicants because statistically, minority applicants are less likely to have wealthy and/or college-educated parents) or which may have discriminatory reputations in minority communities, to expand their pool of applicants to include racial minorities. Second, affirmative action requires that the minority race of an applicant be considered as a positive factor in admissions. This allows colleges and universities to overcome past and current admissions practices that discriminate against racial minorities, and to increase the admission of racial minorities to their schools.

Why is affirmative action used in higher education? Is it widely used?

Prior to the late 1960s, no affirmative action existed in education. Although racial minorities constituted approximately 19 percent of the population of the United States at that time, they were dramatically underrepresented in higher education and, as a result, in professional life. For example, less than 2 percent of all doctors, lawyers, medical students, and law students were racial minorities. As of 1970, two black medical schools, Howard and Meharry universities, had trained more than 75 percent of all minority doctors in the country.

During the late 1960s and early 1970s, colleges, universities, and graduate schools (especially medical and law schools) began to expand student enrollments substantially. Some, but not most, began to adopt and implement affirmative-action admissions programs for three reasons.

First, some institutions of higher education sought to overcome past and current practices that discriminated against racial minorities. They decided that such discrimination was wrong and that they had an obligation to serve all segments of the community, not just whites. Because these schools expanded their enrollment levels, they resolved to give some of their new openings to minority applicants.

Second, some institutions also realized that the grade-point averages and written aptitude tests used as admissions criteria not only discriminated against minority applicants—because of the segregated and inferior public education given to racial minorities for so long—but also did not significantly help with making admissions decisions. Additionally, as noted earlier, some institutions evaluated applicants by criteria clearly unrelated to a student's ability to perform, such as his parents' wealth, and whether his parents were alumni. Since these criteria have a discriminatory impact upon minority applicants, some schools resolved to overcome this pattern by also giving extra weight to the minority status of qualified applicants.

Third, some schools simply believed that providing a genuinely diverse student body, in which all students learn from each other and benefit from a robust exchange of ideas and viewpoints, required the admission of more than a token number of minority students.

Accordingly, many, but not most, institutions of higher education implemented affirmative-action programs during the late 1960s and early 1970s. Some of those programs set aside a minimum number of places in the incoming class for minority applicants, but most simply added race as another of the many positive factors used to make admissions decisions.

Is it lawful to use an affirmative-action admissions program which sets aside a minimum number of admissions for disadvantaged minority applicants and which considers disadvantaged minority applicants separately from all other applicants?

Probably not. In *Regents of the University of California v. Bakke*,[4] the Supreme Court reviewed a medical school's affirmative action admissions program, which set aside 16 out of 100 places for disadvantaged minority students, using different criteria for these applicants than for other applicants. In effect, the school considered disadvantaged minority applicants separately from all other applicants. In a close and confusing vote, the Supreme Court invalidated this program. Justice Powell, whose vote made a majority in *Bakke*, stated that the program would have been lawful if there had been findings of past discrimination by the medical school.

As a result of *Bakke*, is it now lawful and constitutional to use an affirmative-action admissions program which uses race as a positive factor in admitting minority applicants?

For the most part. However, a lower-court decision and an unusual division of votes on the courts has rendered the future of *Bakke* uncertain. Four of the nine judges on the Supreme Court, led by Justice Brennan, voted to uphold the affirmative-action admissions program in *Bakke* as constitutional, and thereby voted to uphold more flexible programs that merely take race into account. Moreover, in a separate opinion Justice Powell stated that flexible programs which take race into account as one of several factors would be constitutional. Educational institutions may seek to create diversity by giving positive consideration to such factors "as geographic origin or life spent on a farm," and similarly, "race or ethnic background may be deemed a 'plus' in a particular applicant's file."

In addition, a recent federal appeals court decision in Texas challenged the use of affirmative action in education and rejected the approach in *Bakke*. Although the Supreme Court turned down the opportunity to review the case, many feel that soon the highest court in the land will take another look at the question of affirmative action in education.

Are affirmative-action programs lawful when no proof of past discrimination has been shown?

Yes. These programs, however, must comply with the guidelines set out in the *Bakke* decision: race or ethnic background provides a "plus" for an applicant during the evaluation process. Race or ethnic background considered alone cannot determine admission.

5

HOUSING

Residential apartheid remains an American reality. Housing discrimination is one of the most widely practiced form of racial discrimination in the United States. This chapter discusses the laws that respond to housing discrimination and the federal court cases that affect housing discrimination.

Before exploring the specifics of housing-discrimination law, it is important to consider the history of housing discrimination in the United States. Much of the discrimination and segregation in today's housing market is a direct product of our government's programs, policies, and legal precedent. For instance, until 1948, our government enforced deeds and land contracts for the sale of housing that prevented future purchasers from selling the property to an African-American. In addition, federal government mortgage insurance and loan programs, until the 1950s, officially encouraged racially homogeneous neighborhoods. Finally, public housing programs, until the early 1960s, provided housing for both racial minorities and whites, but only on a segregated basis. These practices and policies were in place for decades, and it was common practice for the private real-estate and banking industries to follow the government's lead. In light of this history, it is not surprising that many private real-estate brokers still discriminate based on race.

To some extent the federal government has attempted to correct its own history of discrimination through federal laws and court decisions interpreting those laws. They form the core of the arsenal of weapons used to combat housing discrimination.

What are the major federal protections against discrimination in housing?

Three major sources of federal protection guard against discrimination in housing. The first is Title VIII, which is part of the Civil Rights Act of 1968. Title VIII prohibits discriminatory real-estate practices by either government agencies or private individuals. The second source of federal housing protection is the Civil Rights Act of 1866. This act was revived by the Supreme Court in its famous 1968 case, *Jones v. Alfred H. Mayer Co.* Much like Title VIII, the Civil Rights Act of 1866 prohibits discriminatory real-estate practices both by public official and by private individuals. The third protection is the Equal Protection Clause of the Fourteenth Amendment. This prohibits intentional housing discrimination by state and local government agencies.

Are there differences in coverage and enforcement among Title VIII, the Civil Rights Act of 1866, and the Equal Protection Clause?

Yes, there are important differences among the three federal prohibitions.

(1) Title VIII broadly prohibits real-estate discrimination.

However, it contains several exemptions. Title VIII allows someone to sue using three different procedures.

(2) The Civil Rights Act of 1866 is the most sweeping prohibition against real-estate discrimination. Unlike Title VIII, it contains no exceptions or exemptions. The Civil Rights Act of 1866 can be enforced only through lawsuits filed by individuals.

(3) The Equal Protection Clause only prohibits *intentional* discrimination by *government* agencies. Like the Civil Rights Act of 1866, it is enforced only through lawsuits.

PROHIBITED REAL-ESTATE PRACTICES

What types of discriminatory real-estate practices does Title VIII prohibit?

Title VIII provides legal procedures to help replace segregated housing with what Congress calls "truly integrated and balanced living patterns." These laws prohibit discrimination on grounds of race, color, religion, sex, handicap, familial status, or national origin. It is illegal to:

(1) Refuse "to sell or rent," refuse "to negotiate for the sale or rental," or simply to make "unavailable" a dwelling on grounds of race, color, et cetera;

(2) Discriminate in "the terms, conditions or privileges" or in "the provision of services or facilities" when selling or renting a dwelling;

(3) Publish "any notice, statement, or advertisement" indicating a racial limitation or preference in connection with a housing sale or rental;

(4) Represent to any person "that any dwelling is not available for inspection, sale, or rental when such dwelling is in fact so available";

(5) Engage in any "attempt to induce," for profit, any per-

son to sell or rent a dwelling based on the probability of minority persons moving into the neighborhood (blockbusting);

(6) Discriminate "in any sale or rental to any person because of a handicap" or refuse to permit "reasonable modifications of existing premises occupied or to be occupied . . . necessary to afford such person equal opportunity to use and enjoy a dwelling," at the expense of the disabled person. Persons with AIDS or who are HIV-positive qualify as handicapped.

These prohibitions give nondiscrimination rights primarily to prospective buyers and renters. Another section of Title VIII protects the right of minority brokers and agents to participate in any multiple-listing service or real-estate organization.

Are there any real-estate transactions specifically exempted from compliance with the nondiscrimination requirements of Title VIII?

Yes, two major types of transactions are exempt. First, Title VIII exempts the sale or rental of a single-family dwelling by its owner, so long as no real-estate sales or rental services are used and the owner does not own more than three such single-family houses. Second, Title VIII permits discrimination in the rental of rooms or units in a dwelling containing living quarters for no more than four families, so long as the owner actually lives in the dwelling. However, even exempted sellers and renters are prohibited from publishing or causing to be published any notice, statement, or advertisement indicating a racial limitation or preference. Despite these exceptions, about 80 percent of America's housing is covered by Title VIII.

In addition, there are some minor exceptions that have become more important as Title VIII has aged. These exceptions include exemptions for religious organizations and private clubs; certain limitations on the maximum number of occupants who can occupy a dwelling; and exclusion of a person who has been convicted of the manufacture or distribution of an illegal drug.

Are other discriminatory real-estate practices prohibited by Title VIII?

Yes. Title VIII also prohibits banks, building and loan associations, insurance companies, and other businesses that make real-estate loans from engaging in any discriminatory loan denials (for "purchasing, contracting, improving, repairing, or maintaining a dwelling") and any discrimination "in the fixing of the amount, interest rate, duration, or other terms or conditions of such loan or other financial assistance." In addition, Title VIII contains a catchall provision making it unlawful to "intimidate" or "interfere with" any person in connection with the exercise of rights protected by Title VIII.

How does one prove discrimination in the sale of a lot or of a dwelling?

Proof of discrimination follows two steps. First, to establish what is called a "prima facie" case of racial discrimination (meaning *at first view*), the plaintiff must prove only that the conduct of the defendant "actually or predictably results in discrimination." For instance, a minority plaintiff who claims that he has been the victim of a discriminatory denial of housing may establish a sufficient case by proving: (1) that he is black; (2) that he applied for and was qualified to rent or purchase the housing; (3) that he was rejected; and (4) that the housing opportunity remained available.

Second, after the plaintiff shows discrimination, the developer, seller, or agent must give a legitimate nondiscriminatory reason for rejecting the offer; in other words, he must come forward with evidence to show that the rejection was not motivated by considerations of race. The defendant also must demonstrate that no acceptable alternative could have accomplished the same business goal with less discrimination. If the defendant does not present any evidence in response to the plaintiff, then a violation of Title VIII is found and the complainant is entitled to legal relief.

Does Title VIII prohibit unintentional as well as intentional discrimination in real-estate transactions?

Yes. Practices that have a discriminatory *effect* are unlawful under Title VIII, regardless of whether the person practicing them has a discriminatory motive.

In order to establish a violation of Title VIII, must a person prove that race was the *sole* basis for a refusal to rent or sell?

No. A minority person need only show that race was a "significant factor" in the refusal, not that it was the only basis.

Are claims under Title VIII possible only for minority persons?

No. Title VIII prohibits discriminatory practices because of race, color, religion, sex, national origin, or medical disability. Therefore, whites as well as minorities can bring a lawsuit for violation of Title VIII if they are discriminated against on the basis of any of these factors.

Are families, single people with children, and people who are unmarried protected by Title VIII?

Yes. Title VIII prohibits discrimination against families with children and discrimination based on family status. However, landlords can make some restrictions on children for health reasons or to maintain a quiet environment. Some state supreme courts have ruled that landlords who hold certain religious beliefs may have a right to restrict unmarried couples from renting.

Is it also true that people with HIV or AIDS are now protected by Title VIII?

Yes. Even if a person does not have HIV or AIDS, if there is a *perception* that the person has or will get HIV or AIDS, Title VIII applies.

Does a person have to be directly discriminated against to have a claim under Title VIII?

No. Title VIII has two primary goals: to promote integration and to end discrimination. If someone is denied the right to live in integrated housing, there is cause for a claim for both the party excluded and those not excluded who are being denied an opportunity to live in integrated housing. In other words, people with housing in such a situation may sue.

Can a city do anything to stop practices that segregate housing?

Yes. Under Title VIII, a city has the right to sue on its own behalf to promote integration. In addition, most cities and states have separate laws prohibiting housing discrimination, which can give the city a right to sue either on behalf of those denied housing or on its own behalf. The Supreme Court recognizes that integrated housing benefits the entire community, and that when housing is segregated everyone suffers a harm.

What are testers, and how are they used in proving discrimination under Title VIII?

"Testers" are minority persons and white persons—carefully matched in age, income, education, and other characteristics—who do not seek housing for themselves but who apply for a dwelling to "test" its availability. In proving a case of dis-crimination under Title VIII, it is very helpful to have evidence from testers. Proof of discrimination against testers, although helpful, is not necessarily essential. Statistics can also be used to help prove discrimination. For example, some statistics reveal that blacks and Hispanics receive home loans from lend-ing institutions at a much lower rate than whites from similar economic backgrounds. Such data is useful when proving a case of discrimination under Title VII.

What is the scope of the Civil Rights Act of 1866?

Unlike Title VIII, the Civil Rights Act of 1866 is short and straight-forward. Section 1982 of the 1866 act states in one sentence that all citizens "shall have the same right . . . as is enjoyed by white citizens . . . to inherit, purchase, lease, sell, hold and convey real and personal property." Section 1981 of the 1866 act states that all persons "shall have the same right . . . to make and enforce contracts . . . as is enjoyed by white citizens." Despite the breadth of its language, the 1866 act for a hundred years was presumed to apply only to government and not to private discrimination. However, two months after Title VIII was enacted by Congress, the Supreme Court in *Jones v. Alfred H. Mayer Co.* held for the first time that the 1866 act "bars *all* racial discrimination, private as well as public, in the sale or rental of property."[1]

Does the Civil Rights Act of 1866 have exemptions similar to those in Title VIII?

No. The Civil Rights Act of 1866 has no exemptions.

If the prohibitions against discrimination in the 1866 act are broader than in Title VIII, is Title VIII unnecessary?

No. Title VIII provides several advantages to discriminated-against persons that are not in the 1866 act. For example, Title

VIII, unlike the 1866 act, prohibits discriminatory advertising, authorizes remedies besides lawsuits, authorizes the attorney general as well as individuals to sue, and prohibits housing practices that have a discriminatory effect regardless of whether they were intentionally racially discriminatory. Because of these differences, it is important to examine the methods of enforcement both of Title VIII and of the 1866 act.

REMEDIES AND PROCEDURES UNDER TITLE VIII AND THE CIVIL RIGHTS ACT OF 1866

Are there any enforcement procedures that must be followed under Title VIII or under the Civil Rights Act of 1866 in order to obtain the rights guaranteed by those federal statutes?

Yes. Although Title VIII and the 1866 act together prohibit all forms of discrimination, the federal protections and remedies are realized only through enforcement lawsuits. Enforcement under Title VIII requires a private complainant to follow certain administrative procedures within time limitations. Enforcement under the 1866 act, on the other hand, simply requires a suit in court as soon as possible.

Who is authorized to enforce the guarantees of Title VIII?

There are three routes for enforcing the guarantees of Title VIII. First, aggrieved individuals may file complaints with the federal Department of Housing and Urban Development (HUD) or seek administrative enforcement through state and local agencies. This method was significantly strengthened by the 1988 Amendments Act. Second, private individuals are authorized to enforce Title VIII through civil court cases. Third, the attorney general can enforce Title VIII in cases "of general public importance" or where a "pattern or practice" of discrimination is shown to exist. Although housing lawsuits by the attorney general are rare, individuals should make their grievances known to the attorney general and urge that legal action be taken.

What about suing in federal court under Title VIII?

Individual enforcement, that is, suing directly in a federal trial court, must be initiated no later than two years after the alleged act of discrimination. If the person with a discrimination claim cannot afford an attorney, the court may appoint an attorney for such a person. If the court finds that a discriminatory housing practice has occurred or will occur, the court can order that damages be paid, issue temporary or permanent injunctions preventing the defendant from engaging in the practice, or take any other action held to be appropriate.

What are the advantages and disadvantages of going straight to court, as opposed to going through the administrative proceedings under Title VIII?

One advantage of going to court is that the complainant has two years to go to court for a civil case and only one year to go to HUD after the discrimination incident has occurred. Perhaps the biggest advantage is that the court may award unlimited punitive damages and thus there may be greater financial compensation. Unlike a HUD proceeding, a civil case can be held in front of a jury. Some complainants prefer juries because there is a possibility for higher damage awards, especially if the complainant is seen as sympathetic. Other complainants believe that jury trial awards are too erratic and that the HUD administrative law judges are more liberal.

The advantages of going to HUD include avoiding expensive legal fees, especially if the complainant does not receive a court-appointed lawyer; having a HUD lawyer prosecute the complainant's case; and having special proceedings intended to take less time than court cases, which often take years to litigate due to court backlogs.

Can a complainant sue in court while proceeding through HUD at the same time?

Yes. In fact, the wisest course is to proceed under both methods simultaneously—file a HUD complaint while exploring the option of filing a lawsuit within two years of the discrimination incident.

Are courts authorized to appoint an attorney for a complainant who cannot afford a lawyer but who wishes to file suit under Title VIII?

Yes. A court is authorized to appoint an attorney upon "application by a person alleging a discriminatory housing practice or a person against whom such a practice is alleged."

What remedies are available to persons who have been discriminated against in housing in violation of the Civil Rights Act of 1866?

The remedies are very broad. For example, although the 1866 act itself specifies no remedies, the Supreme Court has held that court orders terminating the discrimination and awarding damages (including unlimited punitive damages) are available. Courts also may award attorneys' fees to the prevailing party.

Does a person have to choose whether to bring a housing-discrimination lawsuit under Title VIII or under the Civil Rights Act of 1866?

No. Title VIII and the Civil Rights Act of 1866 provide independent remedies for discrimination in housing. Complainants who file a lawsuit should claim violations of both statutes.

If a complainant fails to follow the procedural and time-limitation requirements of Title VIII, can he or she still bring a lawsuit under the Civil Rights Act of 1866?

Yes. Failure to comply with the procedural requirements under either Title VIII alternative does not affect a complainant's right to sue under the 1866 act to remedy housing discrimination.

Are there procedural requirements that must be complied with before suing a housing discriminator under the Civil Rights Act of 1866?

No. However, the courts have uniformly held that a lawsuit under the 1866 act must be filed within the time period established by state law—a period that varies, depending upon the state, from one year to five or more years, and the time is not extended for any period when an administrative procedure under Title VIII is pending. Therefore, a complainant ordinarily should file a lawsuit under the 1866 act (and under Title VIII's direct litigation method) as soon as possible after the discriminatory action.

EXCLUSIONARY ZONING AND OTHER GOVERNMENTAL DISCRIMINATION

Is discrimination still practiced in the public sector by state and local governments?

Unfortunately and quite obviously, yes. As noted at the beginning of this chapter, federal, state, and local governments are partly responsible for current segregated-housing patterns. Although most of the overtly segregative policies have disappeared, many have been replaced by more subtle policies of discrimination, especially exclusionary zoning policies that keep many suburban communities virtually all-white.

What forms of overt governmental discrimination have been held unconstitutional or otherwise unlawful?

Generally, all forms of overt discrimination are prohibited. Probably the most blatant form of housing segregation ever confronted by the Supreme Court involved local ordinances that prohibited blacks from living in white neighborhoods. As early as 1917, the Supreme Court held that such ordinances violated the Fourteenth Amendment.

Another form of overt segregation involved enforcement by state courts of racially restrictive "covenants." These covenants were contractual provisions that required white purchasers of homes to sell only to other white purchasers. The Supreme Court at first believed these racially restrictive covenants to be an entirely private matter. In 1972, however, a federal court held that it was a violation of Title VIII for a local government even to file a deed with a racially restrictive covenant.

Another form of overt governmental segregation has been the racial designation or "siting" of public housing. This happens when the government either formally designates a public housing project as a black project or places a housing project in the center of a black community. These practices have been held unlawful, whether implemented by local housing authorities or encouraged by the federal government.

Have these various forms of overt housing segregation been reduced?

Yes. However, this is not to say that the days of overt segregation are past. As one court has concluded, "overtly bigoted behavior has become more unfashionable . . . not . . . that racial discrimination has disappeared."[2]

What is racially exclusionary zoning?

Racially exclusionary zoning happens when a local government permits land to be used in such a way that no minorities have access to it. In civil-rights law, exclusionary zoning refers to the use of low-density residential zoning (large expansive lots with big houses and few residents) to the almost total exclusion of other types of residential zoning (for example, small-lot or multi-dwelling, multi-family zoning). Such exclusionary zoning, especially by a virtually all-white community, discriminates against minorities, and hence becomes racially exclusionary, because minorities on average are poorer than whites and are less able to buy or rent low-density housing. It is clear that the types of houses built in a neighborhood will determine, to a large degree, the race of the occupants.

Does racially exclusionary zoning deny minorities equal protection of the law in violation of the Fourteenth Amendment?

Yes, but it is almost impossible to prove it in court. Three major obstacles make proof of unconstitutional discrimination in zoning difficult: the Supreme Court defers to local zoning decisions; narrowly defines who may bring such suits; and requires plaintiffs to prove intentional discrimination on the part of the government.

Is racially exclusionary zoning, regardless of the Fourteenth Amendment, prohibited by Title VIII?

Apparently, yes. Although the Supreme Court has not yet decided this issue, it has declined to review a number of lower court cases that have held that exclusionary zoning is prohibited by Title VIII. The conclusion reached by the lower courts is warranted for a number of reasons: (1) Title VIII applies not just to private entities but also to the government; (2) Title VIII prohibits interfering with Title VIII rights; (3) Title VIII prohibits making a dwelling unit "unavailable" on grounds of race; (4) Title VIII prohibits practices that have a discriminatory effect, regardless of intent; (5) Title VIII was enacted by Congress and has been interpreted by the Supreme Court liberally to allow many different aggrieved parties to sue.

As a federal court recently noted, Title VIII may be a more attractive method than the Fourteenth Amendment for achieving nondiscriminatory housing, since it does not require proof of discriminatory intent.

Are there other possible remedies for racially exclusionary zoning?

Yes. Several state courts have held racially exclusionary zoning to be unconstitutional under state constitutions.

There seem to be several laws to promote integrated housing and to prohibit housing discrimination. Are they enough to end housing segregation and discrimination in the United States?

Unfortunately, no. Housing is as segregated as it was 20 years ago. In a recent study by the government, it was found that African-Americans seeking housing will be discriminated against 40 percent of the time. Although the laws discussed in this chapter are important, they alone will not end housing segregation in the United States.

What else is needed?

Housing opportunities in this country will not be free of discrimination until there is an affirmative effort by the government to end segregation. Opposing exclusionary practices is not enough. Housing opportunities need to be created. The cost of housing cannot be allowed to serve as an excuse to exclude people based on their race or religion. Affirmative efforts to promote integration are necessary, such as making affordable housing available in all parts of communities. The laws we have are an important beginning, but are only a beginning.

6

PUBLIC ACCOMMODATIONS

The modern civil-rights movement, which toppled the more overt forms of racial discrimination, began as an effort to desegregate public accommodations—city buses in Montgomery, Alabama. On December 1, 1955, Rosa Parks, a black woman, refused to yield her seat on a city bus to a white passenger. She was arrested for violating an ordinance requiring segregation in public transportation. In protest over the arrest, a 27-year-old minister named Martin Luther King, Jr., organized a citywide boycott of buses. In the years that followed, his tactic of direct, nonviolent action against segregation was repeated in countless lunch-counter sit-ins, freedom rides, marches, boycotts, and demonstrations. The "movement," as it came to be known, helped change the laws and customs of a nation.

What is a "public accommodation"?

A public accommodation is any establishment that is open to the public, such as a hotel, restaurant, library, train, bus, or tennis court. A less obvious example would be the Boy Scouts.

One court has held that the scouts were a place of public accommodation even though they did not operate in a single place but in a large number of temporary locations.

Does the Constitution prohibit racial discrimination in public accommodations?

Yes. The Fourteenth Amendment prohibits all forms of official racial segregation in public accommodations, whether or not the facilities are actually owned or operated by the state. Purely private acts of segregation, in which there has been no significant state involvement, do not violate the equal protection clause of the Fourteenth Amendment.

The Thirteenth Amendment, unlike the Fourteenth, applies to private as well as official acts. Although it was initially held to prohibit only slavery, the Supreme Court has since ruled that the Thirteenth Amendment prohibits the imposition of "badges and incidents of slavery," such as the refusal of private parties to sell or lease real estate to blacks. The amendment also protects the equal right to contract for services and accommodations, such as the right to join a neighborhood swimming club or enter into an employment contract.

Were the Thirteenth and Fourteenth Amendments effectively enforced after their enactment to prohibit discrimination in public accommodations?

No. Both the Thirteenth and Fourteenth Amendments contain provisions authorizing Congress to pass implementing legislation. Under this constitutional authority, Congress enacted in 1875 the nation's first public-accommodations law. It guaranteed to all persons, without regard to race or color, the full and equal enjoyment of inns, public transportation, theaters, and places of public amusement. Eight years later, the Supreme Court declared the act unconstitutional. It held that the Thirteenth Amendment prohibited slavery, not racial discrimination, and that the Fourteenth Amendment prohibited state, not private, action. Discrimination in privately owned facilities that were open to the general public was therefore not prohibited by the Constitution, the Court ruled.

Was there any response by the states to the Supreme Court's decision?

Yes. In response to the Court's decision, and as part of the restoration of white rule after Reconstruction, many of the states adopted Jim Crow laws requiring segregation of the races in places of public accommodation. No detail of life was too small to be regulated by Jim Crow. Jim Crow laws required segregation in schools, churches, housing, transportation, jobs, prisons, cemeteries, and public buildings. Courts in Atlanta used a Jim Crow Bible to swear in black witnesses. Birmingham had an ordinance making it a crime for blacks and whites to play checkers or dominoes together.

Was Jim Crow ever tested in court?

Yes. In 1896, the Supreme Court decided *Plessy v. Ferguson,* a case challenging a Jim Crow law enacted by the state of Louisiana. Homer Plessy, who was seven-eighths white and one-eighth Negro, was a passenger on the East Louisiana Railway from New Orleans to Covington. He took a seat in the car reserved for white passengers. The conductor directed Plessy to move to the Jim Crow car, which by state law was required to be "equal but separate." Plessy refused to move. He was arrested and charged with the crime of sitting in a coach reserved for whites. Plessy argued that the law was unconstitutional, and that in any event he looked more white than black. His arguments were rejected. The Court held that separate but equal accommodations were constitutional because they existed for the "preservation of the public peace and good order."[1] The Court thus approved official racial segregation in places of public accommodation and allowed the states to adopt Jim Crow as the law of their land.

Plessy v. Ferguson was not the last word on the constitutionality of Jim Crow. In 1954, in *Brown v. Board of Education*, a school desegregation case, the Supreme Court effectively reversed itself and laid Jim Crow to rest. *Brown* was the culmination of a line of cases in which the Court found specific educational facilities and programs for blacks to be unconstitutional because they were not in fact equal. The Court did not expressly overrule *Plessy v. Ferguson*, but it held that "in the field of public education the doctrine of 'separate but equal' has no place."[2]

What practices have been held unconstitutional under *Brown* and the Fourteenth Amendment?

The *Brown* decision was used to ban officially sanctioned racial segregation in buses, parks, hospitals, swimming pools and bath houses, city golf courses, airport restaurants, courtroom seating, municipal auditoriums, prisons and jails, and in virtually every other form in which it came before the courts.

Is it always easy to draw a line between official discrimination in public accommodations prohibited by the Fourteenth Amendment and purely private discrimination beyond its reach?

No. There is no specific formula for determining official discrimination, or "state action," as it is called. Instead, the court looks at all the facts, such as whether the operation of a facility is essentially a public function or whether the state gives or receives any benefit in its operation. If there is significant state involvement, the facility, even if privately owned, is subject to the Fourteenth Amendment's prohibition against racial discrimination.

In a case decided in 1961, for example, the Supreme Court held that the refusal to serve blacks by a privately operated coffee shop located in a parking garage owned by the city of Wilmington, Delaware, was prohibited by the Fourteenth Amendment. The Court reasoned that the city and the coffee shop were like a partnership, and that the shop's racial discrimination was a form of state action.

In a later case the Court held that the refusal of a Moose lodge to serve a black person in its dining room and bar was not state action prohibited by the Constitution. The Court said the lodge was a private club. It was a member of a national fraternal organization, it owned the building in which its activities were conducted, there were well-defined requirements for membership, and only members and their guests were permitted in Moose lodges. Even though the lodge had a license from the state to serve alcoholic beverages, that did not constitute sufficient state involvement to make the lodge's discriminatory practices unconstitutional. The Court did, however, prohibit enforcement of a state law that required the lodge to comply with the provisions of its bylaws and constitution. The Court reasoned that since the provisions were discriminatory, requiring compliance would involve the state in enforcing segregation.

Can a state or municipality close down a place of public accommodation rather than operate it on a desegregated basis?

Yes and no. The Supreme Court held in 1964 that Prince Edward County, Virginia, could not close its public schools and meanwhile contribute to the support of private, segregated white schools. Such conduct merely continued segregation in violation of the Fourteenth Amendment. But in a later case

decided in 1971, the Court held that it did not violate the Fourteenth Amendment for the city of Jackson, Mississippi, to close
its swimming pools rather than operate them on a desegregated basis. The Court reasoned that closing the pools to everybody did not deny any racial group equal treatment of the law.

**Aside from the public-accommodations law of 1875, was
there any other Reconstruction-era legislation barring
private discrimination in public accommodations?**

Yes. The Civil Rights Act of 1866 contained two provisions, now
known as 42 U.S.C. §§ 1981 and 1982, barring discrimination in
public accommodations. Section 1982 protects the equal right to
inherit, purchase, lease, sell, hold, and convey property. Section
1981 protects the equal right to make and enforce contracts.

**Have sections 1981 and 1982 been used extensively
to remedy discrimination in public accommodations?**

No, but the law is changing and the use of the two statutes has
increased. Both laws were presumed for more than a hundred
years to apply only to state action, while Jim Crow, as we have
seen, was long regarded as constitutional. The statutes thus had
no impact on private discrimination in public accommodations.
In 1968, however, the Supreme Court ruled that section 1982,
based in part upon the Thirteenth Amendment, prohibited private discrimination in real-estate transactions. In 1975, it ruled
that section 1981 prohibited private discrimination in the making
of contracts. The effect of these decisions was to prohibit owners
and managers from discriminating in contracting with minorities
for the use of privately owned public accommodations.

**What kinds of practices are subject to challenge
under sections 1981 and 1982?**

A wide variety of discriminatory practices are subject to chal-

lenge under sections 1981 and 1982, such as the refusal of a
hunting and fishing club to admit a black to its membership;
the refusal of a beauty-salon operator to wash and set the hair
of a black patron; a lounge operator's refusal to serve blacks; a
bartender's refusal to sell soft drinks to blacks attending a private party held at a local fraternal organization; and the refusal
of a public cemetery to sell burial plots to blacks.

Do sections 1981 and 1982 exclude any discriminatory practices from coverage?

Neither statute contains any express limitations in coverage.
Arguments have been raised in several cases in the Supreme
Court that the scope of the laws is limited by the right of privacy. According to this argument, certain discriminatory practices, such as those in the home or a similar intimate setting,
are beyond the power of the government to regulate. In the
cases before it, the Court concluded that the setting in which
the discrimination was practiced was public. It had no occa-
sion to decide the privacy issue.

In one of the cases, a community corporation refused to
allow blacks to become members of a park and playground it
operated. The Court found the practice was unlawful under
section 1982, since membership was generally open to all persons living in the neighborhood—except blacks. The corporation was not in fact a private social club, only a racially
exclusive club. The Court reached the same result under section 1982 in a similar case decided four years later involving a
community swimming pool association. The Court has also
held that the statute prohibits a private, commercially operated, nonsectarian school from refusing to contract with and
admit blacks. Lower courts have similarly refused to apply a
privacy or associational exemption to the statutes where the
discrimination was practiced in a public setting— for example,

in a fraternal organization that the court found was simply a drinking club.

Is it necessary to prove that the discrimination was intentional to establish a violation of sections 1981 and 1982?

Yes, if the discrimination is challenged under section 1981. The Supreme Court has held that section 1981 can be violated only by acts that are *intentionally* discriminatory (although the Court said that Congress has the power to make unlawful acts which have a discriminatory *effect* or *result*). In another case, the Court declined to consider whether discriminatory intent was also required for a violation of section 1982.

How are the Thirteenth and Fourteenth Amendments and sections 1981 and 1982 enforced? What remedies do they provide?

The Thirteenth and Fourteenth Amendments are enforced primarily through lawsuits brought by private individuals. Remedies include orders stopping the discrimination and awarding damages and attorneys' fees. The federal government also has authority to prosecute violations of criminal statutes protecting the equal access to public accommodations.

THE INTERSTATE COMMERCE ACT

What is the Interstate Commerce Act? Does it prohibit racial discrimination?

Congress enacted the Interstate Commerce Act in 1887. It established the Interstate Commerce Commission (ICC) to license and regulate rail, bus, and other forms of public transportation (common carriers). The act prohibits common carriers engaged in interstate commerce from subjecting any person to racial discrimination.

Is discrimination affecting only transportation within a state also prohibited by the act?

No. Discrimination that is purely local and has no impact upon commerce between the states or with foreign countries is not subject to regulation by the Interstate Commerce Act. In practice, transportation almost always affects interstate commerce. The subway system in Atlanta, for example, is wholly within the state of Georgia. However, during the 1996 Olympic Games, the subways had an undoubted impact on interstate travel because they carried passengers from around the country and the world from the airport to the various Olympic venues in the city.

Is state action a requirement for certain behavior to be found in violation of the act?

No. The act prohibits discrimination in interstate commerce by private and public carriers whether or not the discrimination is caused by state law or the carrier's own practices.

What kinds of practices have been found discriminatory under the Interstate Commerce Act?

During the early years of its existence, the Interstate Commerce Act was allowed to permit Jim Crow facilities in interstate commerce. In 1941, however, the Supreme Court ushered in a new era in interstate transportation and held that the denial of equal accommodations on a train on the basis of race was a violation of the Interstate Commerce Act.

The act also bans discrimination in terminals and restaurants that are an integral part of the carrier's service for interstate passengers. It is immaterial whether the facilities are actually owned or operated by the carrier itself. A carrier cannot escape its duty to treat all interstate passengers alike, either through segregating its own facilities or using the segregated facilities of others.

How are the antidiscrimination provisions of the act enforced?

The provisions of the act are enforced by filing complaints with the ICC and by lawsuits brought in the federal district courts.

THE CIVIL AERONAUTICS ACT

Is discrimination in air travel also prohibited by law?

Yes. The Civil Aeronautics Act contains a provision patterned after the Interstate Commerce Act prohibiting racial discrimination in air travel. One of the first cases applying this law was brought in 1954 by Ella Fitzgerald, a famous popular singer. She charged that she was discriminated against because of her race when she was denied a reserved seat on a flight from Honolulu to Sydney, Australia, where she was scheduled to give a performance. The district court dismissed Ms. Fitzgerald's lawsuit because it said it had no jurisdiction. The court of appeals reversed and sent the case back for trial, but there is no written opinion of what ultimately happened in the case. The Civil Aeronautics Act has also been used to prohibit segregation in airport terminal facilities.

TITLE II OF THE CIVIL RIGHTS ACT OF 1964

What is Title II of the Civil Rights Act of 1964 and what does it provide?

It is the modern public-accommodations law, and it was enacted by Congress pursuant to its power to regulate interstate commerce. Title II provides that all persons are entitled to the enjoyment of goods, services, and facilities of any place of public accommodation without discrimination on the grounds of race, color, religion, or national origin.

Four classes of business establishment are covered by the act if the establishment is a place of public accommodation and its operations affect commerce. The covered establishments are:

1. Inns, hotels, motels, or other facilities that provide lodging to guests;

2. Restaurants or gasoline stations;

3. Theaters, sports arenas, or other places of entertainment; and

4. Establishments that are located within covered establishments. A barbershop, for example, located in the basement of a hotel which was itself a place of public accommodation, was found to be covered by the act even though 95 percent of the barber's customers were local residents.

Discrimination or segregation required by state or local law is prohibited. No persons may interfere with the right of another to use a covered facility.

Does Title II unreasonably interfere with the right to own and enjoy private property?

No. The Supreme Court held Title II to be constitutional, rejecting the argument that it deprived individuals of their liberty and the right to use their property in any way they choose. The Court noted that 32 states and numerous cities had similar laws and their constitutionality had been upheld, and went on to say that Congress acted properly in light of the difficulties blacks encountered in travel and that government has a responsibility to ease the burdens that discrimination by race placed upon interstate commerce.

May a member of a racial minority be denied access to a place of public accommodation because other patrons might object and the owner lose business?

No. The protection of Title II cannot yield to the prejudices of patrons or the claimed nonracial economic interests of owners and managers. The exclusion of persons from public accommodations because of their race, whatever the asserted justifications, is prohibited.

How is the determination made whether an establishment's operations affect commerce and are covered by Title II?

Commerce is basically trade or travel among the states, the District of Columbia, and any foreign country or territory or possession of the United States. Inns, motels, and similar facilities are deemed to affect commerce if they provide lodging to transient guests. Restaurants, lunch counters, and gasoline stations are covered by Title II if they serve interstate travelers or if a substantial portion of what they sell has moved in commerce. Motion-picture houses and other places of entertainment affect commerce if their films, performers, or other sources of entertainment have moved in commerce. Any establishment located within the premises of a facility that affects commerce is itself covered by Title II.

How much of an effect upon interstate commerce must an establishment have to be covered by Title II?

The effect must be "substantial." However, the success of Title II depends upon the regulation of all establishments that contribute to the problem of racial discrimination in interstate commerce. Thus, Ollie's Barbecue, a restaurant in Birmingham, Alabama, located eleven blocks from an interstate highway, was held in 1964 to be covered by the act because some of the food it served was purchased outside the state and moved through interstate commerce. A billiard parlor in Jacksonville, Florida, that refused to admit blacks was found in 1974 to be subject to Title II as a place of entertainment since its pool tables and cues were manufactured out of state.

What kinds of practices and facilities have been held to be covered by Title II?

Practices and facilities held by the courts to be covered by Title II include: segregation in hotels, motels, YMCA facilities, trailer parks, restaurants, health and beauty spas, bars and package stores, and hospitals; "freedom of choice" seating in dining rooms; a local ordinance prohibiting service at bars to persons in military uniform directed against black servicemen; denial of the use of facilities to blacks at a remote fishing camp, a hunting club, an amusement park, a recreational complex containing boating and swimming facilities, skating rinks, a tournament held on a municipal golf course, a golf course, a beach club, bowling alleys, movie theaters; refusal to serve a white woman at a lunch counter because she was with blacks; refusals to accommodate blacks at beach apartments, a drive-in restaurant, lunch counters, snack bars, a gasoline station and its rest rooms, nightclubs and cabarets, a country club operated by a profit-making corporation, poolrooms, racetracks, and a swimming club.

Are there any exemptions from coverage contained in Title II?

Yes. Title II does not cover private clubs that are not in fact open to the public. It also excludes the so-called "Mrs. Murphy's boardinghouse"—that is, any rooming house with five rooms or less which is occupied by the proprietor as a residence.

May an establishment that serves the general public call itself a private club and escape Title II coverage?

No. A place of public accommodation may not defeat Title II coverage simply by calling itself a private club or even by trying to act like a private club. In determining if a facility is private, the courts look at all the facts and circumstances surrounding its operation. How and why was it created? Is it run for a profit? Who owns it? How has it been operated in the past? Does it have members? If so, how are they chosen? Do they pay dues? Are nonmembers allowed to use the facilities?

In a case in 1969, the Supreme Court was asked to decide if the Lake Nixon Club, a 232-acre privately owned amusement park with swimming, boating, golf, and dancing facilities located outside Little Rock, Arkansas, was a private club. Patrons were required to pay a 25-cent fee and were issued membership cards. The Court reviewed the facts, including that the park had always been segregated and that whites were routinely given, and blacks denied, membership. The Court concluded that Lake Nixon Club was simply a business operated for a profit. It had none of the attributes of self-government and membership-ownership traditionally associated with private clubs.

In a similar case decided in 1973, the Court held that a neighborhood swimming pool in Silver Spring, Maryland, was not a private club. The association that owned the pool granted a preference in membership to anyone living within a three-quarter-mile radius of the pool, except blacks. Aside from the geographical requirement, the only condition for membership was race. The pool was no more private under Title II than the Lake Nixon Club.

Who has the burden of proving whether a club is or is not private within the meaning of the private-club exemption in Title II?

Those complaining of discrimination have the initial burden of establishing a violation of Title II. They must show that an establishment is covered by the act and that it discriminates on the basis of race. Thereafter, the facility must prove by clear and convincing evidence that it is in fact truly private.

How is Title II enforced?

Any person who has been discriminated against in the use of public accommodations can bring suit in federal court. The court can appoint an attorney to represent the person and waive payment of fees and other court costs. The attorney general may intervene if the case is one of general public interest. The attorney general is also authorized to bring suit for an injunction (or court order) prohibiting discriminatory practices where there is reasonable cause to believe that a pattern and practice of discrimination exists.

To encourage individuals injured by racial discrimination to seek judicial relief, Congress has provided that the winning party is entitled to recover costs and reasonable attorneys' fees. Damages are not authorized.

Are the enforcement procedures contained in Title II the sole means of remedying discrimination in public accommodations?

No. Nothing prohibits a person from bringing suit or asserting a right under another law. Thus, a person discriminated against may bring suit under Title II or, for example, under sections 1981 and 1982. Since Title II and sections 1981 and 1982 provide independent remedies for discrimination in public accommodations, a person who files a lawsuit should claim violations of both Title II and sections 1981 and 1982.

Are there advantages to filing a lawsuit under Title II as opposed to sections 1981 and 1982?

There are advantages under both because the remedies provided, and often the scope of coverage, are different. Sections 1981 and 1982 authorize recovery of damages; Title II does not. Title II provides for enforcement by the attorney general and conciliation (or out-of-court settlement) by the Community Relations Service (see below); sections 1981 and 1982 contain no similar provisions. As for scope of coverage, Title II requires effect upon interstate commerce, while sections 1981 and 1982 do not. Section 1881 requires proof of intentional discrimination; Title II does not.

Are there steps that must be taken before an individual can file a lawsuit to enforce Title II?

Yes, in some instances. If a state or local jurisdiction has an agency that can grant relief from discrimination in public accommodations, an individual has to file a complaint with that agency first before bringing a suit in federal court. The purpose of the requirement is to give states and local governments an initial opportunity to correct the discrimination. If they fail to do so after 30 days, the individual is free to file a lawsuit.

How does the Community Relations Service enforce Title II?

The Community Relations Service (CRS) is a federal agency established by the Civil Rights Act of 1964. Its function is to provide assistance to communities in resolving disputes relating to discrimination based on race, color, or national origin. After a lawsuit has been filed to enforce Title II, the court may refer the matter to the CRS for up to 120 days, if the court believes there is a reasonable possibility of obtaining a voluntary settlement.

Can a racial minority who seeks access to a facility covered by Title II be prosecuted for trespass under state law?

No. People threatened with prosecution under state trespass laws because of their peaceful use of public accommodations have a right not even to be brought to trial on such charges. Any charges that are brought may be removed to federal court and there dismissed. The right of removal under Title II is an important one. It prohibits local officials from using state criminal prosecutions to defeat implementation of Title II under the guise of protecting property rights.

TITLE III OF THE CIVIL RIGHTS ACT OF 1964

What is Title III of the Civil Rights Act of 1964?

This is a special public-accommodations law; it authorizes the attorney general to bring suit to stop discrimination in state facilities other than schools or colleges.

How has Title III been used? What is its significance today?

Title III has been used primarily to desegregate prisons and jails. Its main significance is that it allows the attorney general to bring suit and spares private parties the burden and expense of litigation.

STATE LAWS PROHIBITING DISCRIMINATION IN PUBLIC ACCOMMODATIONS

Do states also have laws that prohibit discrimination in public accommodations?

Yes. Most states, many cities, and the District of Columbia have laws prohibiting discrimination on the basis of race or color in places of public accommodation.

Have these state laws been effectively enforced?

Yes and no. Some state courts have been hostile to local public-accommodations laws and have limited their application to exclude such public facilities and organizations as restaurants, dentists' offices, golf courses, apartments, hotels, the Jaycees, the Boy Scouts, and bars. The reasons given for the exclusions were generally that the statutes should be strictly construed and because they interfered with the use of private property.

The Supreme Court, however, has given state public-accommodation laws a broad construction and has upheld them against claims that they interfered with privacy and denied people the right to associate with whomever they wished, a right protected by the First Amendment. In a 1984 case from Minnesota, women successfully challenged their exclusion from the Jaycees under a state law that made it unlawful to discriminate in access to public accommodations because of race, color, creed, religion, disability, natural origin, or sex. The Supreme Court reasoned that the Jaycees were neither small nor select, there were no criteria for judging applicants for membership, and numerous nonmembers regularly participated in organizational activities. The Jaycees lacked the distinctive characteristics (of a family or small neighborhood club, for example) that might have afforded constitutional protection to its decision to exclude a protected group. The Court also held that the state had a compelling interest in eradicating acts of discrimination and that the anti-discrimination law abridged speech or associational freedom no more than was necessary to accomplish that purpose.

In a similar case from California in 1987, the Court held that the state's public-accommodations law prohibited the Rotary Club from excluding a protected group (women) from its membership. The Court has also upheld a New York City law prohibiting discrimination in public accommodations in a case brought by a group of private clubs.

7

FEDERALLY ASSISTED DISCRIMINATION

Institutions or organizations that practice racial discrimination often receive financial assistance from the government. For example, the government provides free textbooks to schools; some of these schools exclude or assign pupils on the basis of race. Sometimes the government grants tax exemptions to all-white private clubs or gives money to support the programs of private and public entities that discriminate. Not only is the underlying discrimination in these instances wrong, but the provision of government assistance to the discriminatory group is also a violation of the law.

This chapter explores the advantages and methods of pursuing various remedies against governmentally assisted discrimination, including seeking termination of federal funding.

Is government assistance to private organizations and institutions very widespread?

Yes. There are three main types of government assistance. The first type of assistance is tax abatement. For example, private clubs and not-for-profit organizations receive substantial government assistance in the form of tax-exempt status and income-tax deductibility of contributions. Tax-exempt status means that the organization pays no taxes. Income-tax deductibility encourages people to donate money to the organizations. The second type of assistance comes in the form of direct grants. Common examples of this type of assistance include public and private schools receiving funding from the Department of Education (DOE); state and local governments receiving public-housing funds from the Department of Housing and Urban Development (HUD); and hospitals receiving substantial grants from the Department of Health and Human Services (DHS). The third type of assistance is government contracts. For example, private companies and institutions of higher education receive large government contracts to build government projects and undertake government research.

THE FIFTH AND FOURTEENTH AMENDMENTS

Do the Fifth and Fourteenth Amendments prohibit government-assisted discrimination?

Yes. The Fourteenth Amendment's Equal Protection Clause prohibits state and local governments from engaging in intentional discrimination. The Fifth Amendment's Due Process Clause prohibits the federal government from engaging in intentional discrimination. These amendments prohibit intentional participation in discrimination by others as well as direct discrimination. This makes sense because government should not be able to discriminate indirectly when it is prohibited from discriminating directly. Generally, all forms of assistance provided to recipients that the government knows or should know are discriminatory are prohibited by the Fifth and Fourteenth Amendment.

Although against government policy, discrimination still occurs because some individuals do not follow the law. Although the government has enacted laws to prevent state and local governments from engaging in intentional discrimination and some forms of unintentional discrimination, discrimination still occurs not only because some people refuse to follow the law, but also because, in many instances, discrimination is difficult to prove.

Can a nonprofit private school that practices racial discrimination because of its religious beliefs be denied tax-exempt status?

Yes. When the government grants a tax exemption, it excuses an entity from paying income tax, and allows persons making a contribution to the entity to take a tax deduction. A tax exemption is justified only if it confers a public benefit. Practicing racial discrimination does not confer a public benefit and is contrary to national public policy. For example, in *Bob Jones University v. United States* (1983), the Supreme Court upheld the denial of tax-exempt status to this university in South Carolina because of its racially discriminatory admissions policy.

How are the Fifth and Fourteenth Amendment prohibitions against unconstitutional government assistance enforced?

Theoretically, each government agency that provides assistance is responsible for ensuring that it does not unconstitutionally aid discriminatory recipients. In practice, however, there is very little constitutional self-enforcement by government agencies. Accordingly, the only effective remedy has been to sue the government agencies that are providing assistance to discriminatory recipients.

Are there any problems facing a person who wants to sue a government agency that is providing assistance to a discriminatory recipient?

Yes. Because such a lawsuit requires significant time and resources, an initial problem will be finding a lawyer who is willing to handle this type of case. Additionally, there are two significant legal problems. First, when suing under the Fifth and Fourteenth Amendments, the person suing has to prove that the agency being sued has engaged in intentional discrimination. Second, although some lawsuits against federal agencies have been successful, many suits have been dismissed because courts have found plaintiffs lacked "standing" to bring the lawsuit. To have "standing" to sue, a plaintiff must show that the federal agency's discriminatory conduct resulted in harm to the plaintiff. Courts have been increasingly reluctant to allow discrimination suits to continue when the claimed injury seems indirect or incidental. For example, if a federal agency prohibited interracial dating in a public school, those individuals who wanted to date interracially would have standing to sue because of the direct harm. Generally, an individual must show more than the fact that he disagrees with the discrimination; he must show direct injury.

Are there any other methods of terminating federal government assistance to discriminatory recipients and challenging their unlawful practices?

Yes. The other methods involve filing lawsuits directly against the recipients and filing administrative charges of discrimination with the federal agencies providing the assistance. For example, a person who has been discriminated against by a private school that receives funding from the Department of Education could report the discrimination directly to the department. Because such agencies are either authorized or required to stop giving financial assistance to discriminating recipients, the filing of an administrative charge may lead to threatened suspension of federal funds and ultimately may convince the recipient to stop discriminating.

TITLE VI OF THE CIVIL RIGHTS ACT OF 1964

What is Title VI of the Civil Rights Act of 1964?

Title VI provides that no person shall be discriminated against on the basis of race, color, or national origin under any program or activity receiving federal financial assistance. As Senator Hubert H. Humphrey explained when Congress was enacting Title VI, "The purpose of Title VI is to make sure that funds of the United States are not used to support racial discrimination."[1] The ultimate sanction under Title VI is to terminate the violator's federal funding.

How broad is the coverage of Title VI?

Fairly broad. Title VI applies to all federal agencies that make grants (there are approximately 30) and prohibits discrimination in any public or private program or activity receiving federal financial assistance. Discrimination is prohibited by Title VI throughout entire institutions or agencies if any part receives federal financial assistance.

In the case of state and local governments, Title VI applies only to the department or agency that receives the federal aid. Where an entity of state or local government receives federal aid and distributes it to another department or agency, both entities are covered.

Title VI is applicable for private corporations, if the federal

113

aid is extended to the corporation as a whole, or if the corporation provides a public service such as social services, education, or housing. If the federal aid is extended to only one plant or geographically separate facility, only that plant is covered.

Are there any exemptions from coverage of Title VI?

Yes. Despite its breadth, there are two significant exceptions. First, Title VI applies only to federal financial assistance. Specifically exempted are contracts of insurance or guarantees in banking programs involving federally insured bank deposits. Second, also exempted are employment practices in any program or activity receiving federal aid unless a primary objective of the financial assistance is to provide employment.

How is Title VI enforced?

The two basic methods of enforcing Title VI are: (1) suits by the attorney general and private parties who have been harmed by the discrimination brought directly against the recipients of federal funds; and (2) administrative investigation and proceedings by federal agencies to terminate funding to discriminatory recipients.

Which federal agencies are required to enforce the nondiscrimination provisions of Title VI?

Title VI applies to every federal department and agency able to give financial assistance through a grant, a loan, or a contract. For example, Title VI applies to the Department of Education, which provides education grants. Each federal department and agency that extends financial assistance is responsible for its own Title VI enforcement. Coordination of the overall Title VI enforcement effort is provided by the Office for Civil Rights of the Department of Justice.

Is it necessary to show that a recipient of federal funds was engaged in intentional discrimination to establish a violation of Title VI, or is it sufficient to show that the recipient's practice had a discriminatory effect?

The Supreme Court has held that it is not necessary to show intentional discrimination to prove a violation of Title VI. Practices that have the effect of discrimination also violate the statute.

What remedies are available to the plaintiffs in Title VI lawsuits against recipients of federal funds?

In lawsuits brought by private parties, the prevailing plaintiffs are entitled to declaratory and injunctive relief. This means the court will issue a declaration that the discrimination is unlawful, will order that the behavior stop (injunctive relief), and, at least where the discrimination was intentional, will order that the wrongdoer pay back pay and monetary damages (to compensate for the damage done). In suits by the attorney general, the government is also entitled to declaratory and injunctive relief. This means that the court will terminate the violator's federal funding. The court can also force the violator to repay the misspent funds.

Must a litigant exhaust any administrative remedies before bringing a Title VI claim in federal court?

No. Federal courts have held that a litigant need not pursue any administrative remedies prior to bringing a suit in court against a recipient of federal funds to enforce Title VI.

How do federal agencies enforce Title VI?

There are two basic methods by which federal agencies ensure that their funding activities comply with Title VI. First, an administrative charge against a recipient filed by or on behalf of a person or class alleging discrimination prompts a federal agency investigation of the alleged discrimination. Second, the agency itself—on its own initiative or in response to a large number of charges—may start a thorough compliance review of the recipient's practices. With either method, the federal agency investigates the recipient and makes a finding of discrimination (noncompliance with Title VI) or of no discrimination (compliance with Title VI).

Since most federal agencies do not initiate Title VI enforcement of their own accord, it is very important that administrative charges of discrimination be filed with the appropriate federal agencies. For example, all public schools and nearly all public and private institutions of higher education receive substantial federal financial assistance from the Department of Education. Accordingly, a person who has been discriminated against by a school should send an administrative charge of discrimination to the Office for Civil Rights of the U.S. Department of Education in Washington, D.C., or to any regional office of the department.

What are the requirements for filing an administrative charge of discrimination with a federal agency under Title VI?

An administrative charge under Title VI is not a formal legal document. A letter is sufficient. The letter should fully describe the nature of the discrimination, and name the institution and the individuals who have committed the discrimination. The letter should be mailed to the appropriate federal agency as soon as possible and not later than 180 days after the discrimination occurred.

What happens once an agency determines that a recipient has engaged in discrimination?

After an agency makes a determination of discrimination, it

must take several steps. First, it must seek to obtain voluntary compliance with Title VI from the recipient. This means that the recipient must be given an opportunity to stop its discrimination, rather than having its federal assistance stopped. Second, if voluntary compliance is not achieved, the agency then must start administrative hearings to terminate the federal assistance, or the agency may refer the matter to the attorney general at the Department of Justice for a lawsuit against the recipient. Third, if the agency decides to terminate funding, it must file a report of the circumstances and grounds for the proposed action with the appropriate House or Senate Committee. Termination becomes effective 30 days after the filing of the report.

Once a person files a complaint with a federal agency, the agency has the responsibility to enforce Title VI. There is nothing else for the individual to do. It might be helpful, however, to write a letter to the agency once in a while to remind the federal officials that action is expected.

Can a recipient appeal a decision to terminate its funds?

Yes. A recipient of federal funds can appeal the decision of an agency to terminate its funding by filing a petition for review in the court of appeals.

Do the federal agencies extending financial assistance have good reputations for enforcing Title VI?

Their reputations are uneven. Enforcement of Title VI has often been ineffective because the various federal agencies charged with enforcement have been an integral part of the discriminatory system. Not only have they resisted civil-rights goals, but they have often viewed such goals to be against their agency's self-interest or have argued that they had no authority to end the discrimination. One court, for example, strongly

117

criticized HUD for failing to prohibit segregation and for having an attitude of "amiable apartheid" in funding racially segregated public housing.[2]

Given the uneven record of civil-rights enforcement by federal agencies providing financial assistance, is it really worth the time and effort to file administrative charges against those who discriminate?

Yes. The administrative procedure for terminating federal assistance is still recommended as a way for individuals to assert their civil rights to equal treatment under the law. And the filing of an administrative charge is a very easy step to take since it only involves sending a letter to the appropriate federal agency.

Are there any advantages to litigation as opposed to seeking an administrative remedy for a violation of Title VI?

Yes. Title VI does not provide a mechanism by which a claimant can actually participate in the administrative process beyond writing a letter of complaint. Moreover, even a finding of a violation by an administrative agency may not include relief for the individual claimant. Litigation may under some circumstances be a better route than filing an administrative complaint since it allows the injured individual to collect monetary damages.

THE JUSTICE SYSTEM IMPROVEMENT ACT OF 1984

What is the Justice System Improvement Act of 1984?

The Justice System Improvement Act of 1984 (JSIA) created a number of federal programs and agencies—including the

National Institute of Justice (NIJ), the Bureau of Justice Statistics (BJS), and the Bureau of Justice Assistance (BJA)—to assist and improve national, state, and local law enforcement. To further these goals, the NIJ, BJS, and BJA are authorized to make grants (in the millions of dollars) to private and public entities, such as state law enforcement and rehabilitation agencies, police departments, and correctional facilities.

Does the JSIA prohibit discrimination in programs or activities funded under the act?

Yes. The JSIA, in addition to being subject to Title VI, is an example of a statute that contains separate provisions for prohibiting discrimination in federally assisted programs. The act provides that no person shall be discriminated against or denied employment on the basis of race, color, religion, national origin, or sex, in any program or activity funded in whole or in part under the act.

How are the nondiscrimination provisions of the JSIA enforced?

The Office of Justice Programs (OJP), a coordinating agency created by the JSIA, enforces the nondiscrimination provisions administratively. The attorney general and aggrieved private parties may also bring lawsuits to enforce the JSIA.

Under what circumstances can payment of suspended funds be resumed?

Payment of suspended funds can be resumed if (1) the affected state or local unit of government enters into a compliance agreement with the OJP and the attorney general; (2) a federal or state court or administrative agency has found the recipient to be in compliance; or (3) the OJP concludes after a hearing that it cannot determine noncompliance.

Must a private party exhaust any administrative remedies before filing suit?

Yes. Prior to filing a lawsuit, an aggrieved party is required to file an administrative complaint with the OJP or other appropriate administrative enforcement agency.

Do the civil-rights enforcement provisions of the JSIA differ from those in Title VI?

Yes. The civil-rights enforcement provisions of the JSIA are different from those in Title VI, in that they require investigations, determinations of noncompliance or compliance, and suspension and termination of funding—all within set time periods. There is also no exemption, as there is in Title VI, for employment discrimination.

Before finding a violation of the JSIA, does the OJP have to make a finding of intentional discrimination?

No. The JSIA prohibits discrimination that has a discriminatory effect, as well as that which has a discriminatory purpose.

Have the OJP and its predecessors done a good job investigating charges and making determinations of discrimination?

Not particularly. During the early years of its existence, the predecessor of the OJP did a poor job of enforcing the anti-discrimination provisions of the law. Because of this poor record, Congress amended the act to require termination of federal funding to discriminatory recipients.

8

JURY SELECTION AND TRIALS

There has been a lot of racial discrimination in the administration of justice in the United States. Courtrooms and prisons and jails used to be segregated. Minorities were not allowed to serve on juries and were denied jobs in law enforcement. Because they were denied admission to many colleges and law schools, minorities had little chance to become lawyers, judges, or prosecutors. As a result of being excluded from participating in the system of justice, minorities were denied the protection of the law. They were also frequently the victims of the law.

How are juries selected?

Jury selection varies from state to state, but generally involves several common, distinct steps. Selection officials, often known as jury commissioners, meet periodically and compile lists of persons eligible to serve on juries. Eligible persons are those who meet age, residency, and similar requirements that might be imposed under state law. State laws may exempt from jury duty those with disabilities, critical employment, or who have personal hardships. In compiling the jury lists, the commissioners use voter rolls, telephone directories, or similar sources of names. The names on the lists are placed on pieces of paper and put in separate boxes for grand and trial juries. Grand juries are used primarily to indict, or charge, persons with the commission of crimes. Grand juries may also investigate the operations of local government and issue reports of their findings. Trial juries hear and decide civil and criminal cases. Names are drawn from the jury box as they are needed for particular terms of court and are placed on lists, or venires. The parties in a particular case select their jury from the names on the venire.

CONSTITUTIONAL PROTECTION AGAINST DISCRIMINATION IN JURY SELECTION

Does the Constitution protect against racial discrimination in jury selection?

Yes. The Sixth Amendment, which applies only to criminal trials, guarantees a defendant the right to a jury selected from a fair cross section of the community. The Fourteenth Amendment, which is broader in scope and prohibits all forms of intentional discrimination by state officials, also protects the right to a representative jury. In addition, it guarantees the right of "equal protection," or treatment, in being selected for jury service.

Why is discrimination in jury selection harmful?

There are many reasons. In an 1880 case, the Supreme Court reversed the conviction of a black man by a West Virginia court because state law didn't allow blacks to sit on his jury. In doing so, the Court said the state law was stigmatizing to the defendant (that is, designed to disgrace or discredit him) and "a stimulant to that race prejudice which is an impediment to securing . . . equal justice" in violation of the Fourteenth Amendment.[1]

People eligible for jury service are found throughout society, and not simply among members of a particular racial or ethnic group. Moreover, the jury is a democratic institution that derives its legitimacy from the fact that it is representative of the community. To allow the exclusion of racial minorities would establish the jury as an instrument of a racial elite and would undermine it as an institution of democratic government. Discrimination in jury selection also destroys the appearance of fairness and brings into question the integrity of the entire judicial process.

How does a criminal defendant establish a violation of the fair cross section requirement of the Sixth Amendment?

A defendant must show several things: that the excluded group is "distinctive" (for example, the Supreme Court held in 1979 that women met this standard because they "are sufficiently numerous and distinct from men"); that the group's representation on the venires from which juries are selected is not fair and reasonable in relation to the number of such persons in the community; and that the underrepresentation is caused by the particular jury-selection process used. When a defendant establishes these facts, the exclusion is deemed unconstitutional, unless the state can prove that attaining a fair cross section would be incompatible with a significant state interest—for example, that a disproportionate number of members of the underrepresented group were entitled to and had claimed exemptions from jury duty.

Must the defendant be a member of the excluded group to raise a Sixth Amendment fair cross section claim?

No. The Sixth Amendment entitles a criminal defendant to a jury drawn from a fair cross section of the community, whether or not he is a member of the excluded group.

How is a violation of the Fourteenth Amendment in jury selection established?

A person can prove a violation of the Fourteenth Amendment by direct evidence of intentional discrimination in jury selection, such as statements by those in charge of making up the jury lists that they didn't think blacks or women were smart or experienced enough to serve on juries. A violation can also be shown by establishing a prima facie case (or presumption of) discrimination by statistical evidence showing the substantial underrepresentation of a distinct class over a period of time. The assumption is that if the disparity is large enough, it did not occur by accident or chance, but race or other class-related factors played a part in selection. A presumption of discrimination created by statistical evidence can be supported by evidence that selection procedures are susceptible of abuse or are not racially neutral—for example, that the officials making up the lists were mainly white and that they included only those people whom they personally knew or who they thought would make "good" jurors. The burden then shifts to the defendant to rebut the challenger's case and show that no discrimination in fact occurred.

What kinds of intentional discrimination have been found to violate the Fourteenth Amendment?

The early cases, such as the one from West Virginia, involved total exclusion. Later decisions make clear that any purposeful discrimination against minorities in jury selection violates the

Fourteenth Amendment. Examples of practices found to be unconstitutional include the token inclusion or restriction of the number of minorities on lists of persons eligible for jury duty; the selection of jurors from segregated tax digests (the names of white property owners were kept on one list and black property owners on another); placing the names of white jurors on white slips of paper and the names of black jurors on yellow slips of paper so that whites could be identified and drawn out of the box for jury service; assigning blacks to special jury panels; and placing blacks at the end of jury lists so that they would be called last, if at all.

How large must a disparity in minority representation on juries be to establish a probable violation of the fair cross section standard of the Constitution?

In general, disparities between minorities in the population and minorities summoned for jury duty in excess of 10 percent would establish a probable violation of the fair cross section standard under the Sixth or Fourteenth Amendments. The courts have not, however, adopted a single formula or standard for measuring underrepresentation in all jury selection cases. Instead, they have looked at the particular facts of each case, taking into account the size of the minority group relative to the general population and other relevant factors.

Is it easy for local officials to rebut a prima facie showing of intentional discrimination in jury selection?

No. Once a prima facie case, or presumption of discrimination, is established, selection officials then have the burden of proving that selection procedures were racially neutral. Mere protestations of good faith that no discrimination was practiced are not sufficient to rebut a prima facie case. Otherwise, the right to equal service upon juries would be illusory, for public officials can hardly be expected to admit to violations of the law. Neither the administrative convenience of jury commissioners nor their personal notions about who might be willing to serve have been found adequate to overcome a prima facie case. Jury officials have a duty not to operate a system that in fact excludes minorities. Rebuttal might be made, however, by showing that the underrepresented group was not eligible for jury duty because of age or similar disqualification.

Which racial minorities are protected from discrimination in jury selection?

In order to claim the protection of the Fourteenth Amendment, a group must establish that it is a recognizable, distinct class, singled out for different treatment under the law. Applying this test, the Supreme Court has found African-Americans and Mexican-Americans to be clearly identifiable racial classes. Lower federal and state courts have found other racial groups entitled to equal-protection status including Puerto Ricans, non-Caucasians (natives of Hawaii and those of Portuguese, Spanish, Italian, Chinese, Japanese, Puerto Rican, and Filipino stock), Native Americans, and those with Spanish-sounding names.

May jury commissioners impose their own standards in selecting jurors?

No. Selection officials may not use standards different from those prescribed by law, even though their motives may be to choose those who they think would be "the best" jurors or to excuse people for whom service would be inconvenient.

May jury commissioners use source lists for jurors which underrepresent minorities?

No source list may be used for juror selection which is discriminatory or which fails reasonably to reflect a cross section of the population. Voter-registration lists have been approved as the sole or primary source for jurors, even though they underrepresented minorities and even in jurisdictions in which there has been a long history of discrimination in registering and voting. The courts have reasoned that there is no violation of the fair cross section requirement where the underrepresentation is caused by a group's failure to register to vote. An additional justification for using voter lists has been that they are among the most broadly based lists available. Since passage of the National Voter Registration Act, which made it far easier for people to register, the use of voter lists should present few problems today.

Must individual grand and trial juries exactly reflect the various minority groups in the population?

No. As long as juries are drawn from a fair cross section of the community, there is no requirement under the Constitution that jurors actually chosen for particular cases must exactly mirror the community and reflect all the various racial groups in the population.

How are constitutional challenges raised to discrimination in jury selection?

Challenges may be raised in civil suits by those who have been excluded from jury service because of their race. Parties, or potential parties, in civil cases who desire representative cross-sectional juries may also bring challenges. Criminal defendants can complain of jury discrimination at their trials or in post-conviction proceedings. Members of groups included on jury lists should also have standing to complain of the exclusion of minorities because of the unequal burden of jury service such practices cast upon them.

What are the remedies for discrimination in jury selection?

Parties in civil cases are entitled to court orders prohibiting the continuation of discrimination and requiring officials to recompile jury lists to fairly represent a cross section of the community. Successful plaintiffs can also recover attorneys' fees from the state defendants.

Criminal defendants who prove racial discrimination in selection of their juries are entitled to have the indictments against them dismissed and their convictions reversed. They may be reindicted and retried, but only by juries that are selected in a constitutional manner.

Is a criminal defendant required to show actual prejudice—that he or she was in fact harmed—to be entitled to a new trial where racial minorities have been excluded or underrepresented in trial jury selection?

No. The Supreme Court has held that constitutional protection is denied by circumstances that create the likelihood or the appearance of bias in the trial of a case. Illegal jury-selection procedures cast such doubt on the integrity of the judicial process that convictions secured in violation of constitutional standards may not stand, whether or not there was a showing of actual prejudice in a particular case.

Is discrimination in grand-jury selection rendered harmless by a defendant's subsequent trial and conviction by a properly constituted trial jury?

No. There is an overriding need to eliminate discrimination in grand jury proceedings. In addition, it is very difficult to determine the effect of bias or discrimination on the decision to indict or charge a person with the commission of a crime. As a result, the Supreme Court has held that discrimination in the selection of the grand jury is not cured by a subsequent trial before a properly constituted trial jury. The defendant's remedy in such a case is reindictment and retrial by grand and trial juries that have been selected in conformity with the Constitution.

Is there a particular time during a criminal proceeding when the issue of discrimination in grand- and trial-jury selection must be raised?

Yes. In federal prosecutions, challenges to the grand jury must be raised by motion prior to trial. If the motion is made after trial, the defendant is deemed to have waived objection except for "cause." Cause is a technical term that means the defendant had a legally valid excuse for not objecting. In addition to showing cause, the defendant must also show the case was actually prejudiced by the discrimination in grand-jury selection.

Most states have similar procedural rules requiring criminal defendants to make prompt objections to any defects in their trials. These state rules have been upheld by the Supreme Court with the result that any error in the trial, including discrimination in grand and trial jury selection, is deemed waived unless the defendant can show both cause and prejudice.

Is it difficult to show cause and prejudice for failing to raise the issue of jury discrimination in a timely manner?

Yes, but not impossible. The courts have indicated that cause for failing to object to jury discrimination in a timely manner would exist where the defendant's attorney was incompetent or physically incapacitated; where the underlying facts or the legal basis for a challenge were reasonably unknown; where state officials interfered in some way with the defendant's ability to raise an objection prior to trial, or to prevent a miscarriage of justice, that is, the conviction of one who is actually innocent. Prejudice, or harm, can be shown from the fact of intentional discrimination in jury selection and from the likelihood that the outcome of the trial would have been different but for the claimed error.

Are courtroom practices such as segregated seating and refusing to use "Mr.," "Mrs.," or "Ms." when addressing minorities permissible?

No. Segregation in seating and other discriminatory courtroom practices, such as referring to black witnesses and defendants solely by their first names, violate equal protection under the Fourteenth Amendment.

May a decision to prosecute ever be based on a person's race?

No. The courts have repeatedly held that while the prosecution has broad discretion, it may never decide to prosecute merely because a person is a member of a racial minority.

May race be used in determining guilt or sentence?

Not if race is being considered in a discriminatory manner. Historically, state laws made race a factor in determining guilt or punishment. During the days of legal segregation, it was generally a crime to integrate trains, buses, prisons, and jails. But in no situation was race more crucial in determining guilt or sentence than in violations of laws regulating sexual conduct and marriage. Alabama, for example, had one statute that punished sex (other than between husband and wife) between members of the same race by imprisonment for six months but had another statute punishing sex between members of different races by imprisonment for two to seven years. Such statutes were initially upheld in 1883 by the Supreme Court on the grounds that all persons, black or white, who committed violations were punished the same. Eighty-one years later, however, the Court rejected such a narrow view of equal protection and invalidated a Florida statute that made it a crime for an interracial couple to occupy the same room at night. The Court found no compelling justification for the racial classification and held it to be invidious discrimination forbidden by the Fourteenth Amendment.

In 1967 the Court struck down a Virginia law that made interracial marriage a crime. It held that even though the law applied to both blacks and whites, it was still a racial classification and was prohibited by the Fourteenth Amendment. The definition of criminal conduct could not be made to turn on the color of a person's skin or that of his or her spouse.

Is a sentence unconstitutional if the defendant shows by statistical evidence that racial considerations may have entered into the deliberations of the jury?

No. The problem of racial discrimination in sentencing has been very difficult to remedy. Race has often made the difference in sentences handed down in cases involving black defendants and white victims. One of the most documented instances of this was use of the death penalty against blacks for the crime of rape. Although more than half of all convicted rapists were white, of 455 men executed for rape since 1930, 405 (nearly 90 percent) were black. (In 1977 the Supreme Court ruled that the death penalty for rape was cruel and unusual punishment in violation of the Eighth Amendment.)

Blacks have also been disproportionately executed for other crimes, such as robbery, assault when serving a life term in prison, and burglary. Of 3,984 persons executed for all crimes since 1930, 2,113 were black—more than 50 percent of the total and five times the proportion of blacks in the population. While the rate of crime among blacks is higher than among other groups, numerous studies have documented that the higher execution rate of blacks is also due to the operation of racial factors in the capital-sentencing scheme. No court, however, has ever held that a statistical showing of discrimination would render unconstitutional the death penalty in a given case.

STATUTORY (AS OPPOSED TO CONSTITUTIONAL) PROTECTION AGAINST DISCRIMINATION IN JURY SELECTION

Are there any federal criminal statutes enacted by Congress that protect minorities from discrimination in jury selection?

Yes. An early federal law, enacted in 1875, makes it a crime for a person who has the duty of selecting or summoning jurors to exclude persons from jury service in any state or federal court because of race or color. The penalty for violating the law is a fine of not more than $5,000.

A later law enacted as part of the Civil Rights Act of 1968 makes it a crime to interfere willfully with someone who has served as a juror—for example, by threatening or injuring him because of how he decided a case. Those convicted of violating the statute may be fined up to $10,000 or imprisoned up to life.

Have the criminal laws against jury discrimination been effectively enforced?

No. In spite of the great amount of jury litigation in the courts and the admitted discrimination that has occurred against minorities, there has been only one reported prosecution under the 1875 act. A Virginia state judge was charged in 1878 for refusing to consider blacks for jury duty in his court. In that case, the Supreme Court upheld the act as a proper exercise of congressional power under the Fourteenth Amendment.

Are there any federal civil statutes designed to protect minorities from discrimination in jury selection?

Yes, the Federal Jury Selection and Service Act of 1968. The Federal Jury Act provides that all litigants have the right to grand and trial juries in the federal courts selected at random from a fair cross section of the community. It also provides that all citizens have the opportunity for consideration for jury service. The act prohibits exclusion of any person from service on juries in federal courts on account of race, color, religion, sex, national origin, or economic status. Each federal trial court is required to devise a written plan for random selection of jurors designed to achieve the objective of representativeness.

Is there a constitutional, as opposed to a statutory, requirement that juries be randomly selected in addition to representing a cross section of the community?

No. Random selection is required for federal juries by the Federal Jury Act, but there is no separate, constitutional requirement that either federal or state juries be randomly selected.

How is the Federal Jury Act enforced?

The Federal Jury Act is enforced by parties to federal trials and by the attorney general of the United States. Either may file motions in civil or criminal cases to dismiss or stay the proceedings on the grounds of "substantial failure" to comply with the provisions of the act. The motion must be accompanied by a sworn statement of facts describing the failure to comply and must be filed before the *voir dire* (examination of jurors) begins or within seven days after the noncompliance was discovered.

Are all failures of selection officials to comply with the Federal Jury Act deemed substantial and thus unlawful?

No. Mere technical violations of the act or those that involved good-faith efforts to comply and do not frustrate the goals of the act are not regarded as "substantial."

In addition to showing substantial noncompliance with the Federal Jury Act, must a challenger also show prejudice or show that the violation tended to exclude some racial group?

No. Congress, in passing the act, was more concerned that regular procedures be established to ensure that juries were representative than that individual challengers show actual prejudice arising from statutory violations.

What are the remedies for noncompliance with the Federal Jury Act?

The only remedies for noncompliance are: (1) a court order staying the proceedings, pending selection of a new grand or trial jury; or (2) an order dismissing the indictment.

Are the procedures in the Federal Jury Act the sole means of attacking constitutional infirmities in jury selection?

No. The Federal Jury Act specifically provides that nothing precludes a person from pursuing other remedies for discrimination in jury selection. The statute is not, therefore, the only way to enforce the Constitution's ban on race discrimination.

ADDITIONAL PROTECTIONS AGAINST RACIALLY BIASED TRIALS

Does a defendant have the right to question prospective jurors prior to trial to determine if they might be racially biased?

Yes, where there is a significant likelihood that racial prejudice might affect the trial or where other special circumstances are present. The right, called the right of voir dire, is based on the Sixth and Fourteenth Amendments, which guarantee a fair and impartial jury.

The right of voir dire is not absolute. In a 1973 case, the defendant claimed that South Carolina police officers had framed him on a narcotics charge in retaliation for his civil-rights activities. Under these circumstances, the Supreme Court held it was error not to allow the accused to ask prospective jurors questions about racial prejudice. In another case, the Court found special circumstances requiring voir dire directed to possible racial prejudice where the crime charged was inter-racial and was a capital offense. In a third case from Massachu-setts, however, in which the only racial factor was assault by a black on a white security guard, the Court held that a general inquiry into the impartiality of potential jurors was sufficient. No specific questions related to race were required to be asked.

What remedy does a defendant have if a prospective juror admits to having racial bias?

If a potential juror admits to racial bias that would prohibit rendering a fair and impartial verdict, then the juror is disqual-ified for "cause" and must be excused by the court. A juror may also be disqualified from serving who has a financial or other special interest in the outcome of the litigation.

What remedy does a defendant have if a prospective juror is merely suspected of being prejudiced?

Jurors who deny racial bias, and whom the court refuses to excuse for cause, may still be dismissed by a party through exercise of so-called "peremptory challenges." Peremptory challenges can be used for any reason—for example, simply because a defendant thinks a juror would favor the prosecution. There is no constitutional right to peremptory challenges, but their use is provided in all jurisdictions and is deeply rooted in our jury system.

Do both sides get peremptory challenges? How many?

Yes, both sides get them. In federal felony trials, the defendant gets ten and the prosecution six peremptory challenges. In misdemeanor trials, each side is entitled to three peremptory challenges. The practice in state courts varies.

May a prosecutor use peremptory challenges to exclude blacks from service on a particular jury panel?

No. In a 1986 case, the Court ruled that it was a violation of the Fourteenth Amendment for a prosecutor to exclude minority jurors in a particular case because of their race. Such a rule was necessary, according to the Supreme Court, to strengthen respect for our system of criminal justice and to ensure that no citizen was disqualified from jury service because of race.

Must the defendant be a member of the excluded group to complain about the misuse of peremptory challenges?

No. Any defendant may challenge the discriminatory use of peremptory challenges based on the Fourteenth Amendment.

Has the discriminatory use of peremptory challenges by the prosecution been widespread?

Yes. According to the Supreme Court, the practice of peremptorily eliminating blacks from trial juries in cases with black defendants has been, and remains, widespread.

What is a defendant's remedy for the discriminatory use of peremptory challenges?

The Supreme Court has held that upon a finding of discrimination, the trial court should either: (1) discharge the venire and start jury selection all over again; or (2) prohibit the continued use of the discriminatory challenges and resume selection with the improperly challenged jurors reinstated.

How does a defendant go about raising a claim of misuse of peremptory challenges?

A defendant must raise any objections to a prosecutor's discriminatory use of challenges in a timely manner, *i.e.*, as soon as the misuse becomes apparent and no later than before the jury is sworn. Otherwise, the right to challenge the discrimination may be deemed waived.

How does a defendant prove discrimination in the prosecution's use of peremptory challenges?

To establish a prima facie case of discrimination, the defendant must show that the prosecutor exercised strikes to remove persons of one race or ethnicity from the jury. Proof of these and any other relevant facts—such as evidence of a pattern of strikes against other minorities or the prosecution's questions during the voir dire examination—raises an inference of purposeful discrimination. The burden then shifts to the prosecution to prove a racially neutral reason for striking the minority jurors. The prosecution need not show that a challenged juror was in fact biased or should have been excused for cause. However, mere denials of discrimination, or statements that the challenged jurors would be partial to the defendant because of their shared race, would be insufficient to rebut a prima facie case. The trial judge must determine, based upon all the evidence, if the defendant has established purposeful racial discrimination.

What kind of evidence should the court consider?

The Supreme Court has said that the pattern of strikes against minority jurors and the prosecution's questions and statements during the voir dire examination are examples of relevant evidence of discrimination. Other courts have identified additional factors: whether the prosecution challenged white jurors on grounds similar to those used to challenge minority jurors; whether the reasons given for striking minority jurors were related to the case; whether the challenged juror was asked meaningful questions; whether the explanation given in fact applied to the challenged juror; and whether the prosecution used fewer than all its peremptory challenges. One court has said that the central question is one of comparability. If blacks are struck for a stated reason but similarly situated whites are not, then the stated reason is racially suspect.

Has it been difficult in practice for the prosecution to meet its burden of rebuttal?

Yes and no, depending on the court in which the claim has been heard. Although the Supreme Court has said that the prosecution's explanation of nondiscrimination must be clear and reasonably specific, it has also held that unless a discriminatory intent is inherent in the prosecutor's explanation, the reason offered will be deemed race-neutral. In practice, some courts have tended to accept any reason offered by the prosecution, provided it was not overtly racial. Others have been more exacting.

May a defendant, as opposed to the prosecution, use peremptory challenges to exclude members of a racial group?

No. The Supreme Court has held that allowing a defendant in a criminal prosecution to exclude jurors on the basis of their race makes the court a participant in a discriminatory scheme and undermines the foundation of our system of justice.

Can a private civil litigant challenge the use of peremptory challenges to exclude persons from jury service on account of race?

Yes. The action of a private party in a civil action in using peremptory challenges in a racially discriminatory manner has been held to be a form of state action in violation of the Fourteenth Amendment.

Are there other remedies, in addition to voir dire, for combating an atmosphere of racial prejudice at trial?

Yes. The courts have recognized that questioning potential jurors, no matter how searching, cannot neutralize all racial bias jurors might have. Accordingly, defendants may move for a change of venue (place of trial) to a site less affected by prejudice or request postponement of trial until prejudicial feelings may have subsided.

The Supreme Court has also indicated that if a conviction is so permeated by racial feelings that it is the result of an "irresistible wave of public passion," it violates the Constitution and must be set aside.[2] Very few cases could meet such a strict standard or overcome the problem of waiver in going to trial without having first sought to neutralize prejudice through a venue change.

What are the standards for determining whether to grant a change of venue?

A change of venue, based upon the Constitution's guarantee of an impartial jury, should be granted where there is a reasonable likelihood of prejudice if the trial is held at the scheduled site.

When must a request for change of venue be made?

In federal trials, a motion for change of venue must be made before the plea is entered or within a reasonable time thereafter as allowed by the court. Similar rules exist in state courts.

How can a defendant prove the likelihood of prejudice to gain a venue change?

A likelihood, or presumption, of prejudice may be shown in various ways: by evidence of bias in the community; pretrial publicity such as assertions of guilt in the media; and publication of alleged confessions, prior criminal record, allegations of bad character, or evidence in the case. Pretrial publicity generated by the prosecution is regarded as especially prejudicial because of the credibility likely to be attached to it. Evidence of the absence of prejudice in the surrounding jurisdictions should also be developed to assist the court in locating an alternate site for trial.

Is it easy in practice to show that pretrial publicity might deprive, or has deprived, a defendant of the right to a fair trial before an impartial jury?

No. The burden of showing the likelihood of prejudice from pretrial publicity is an extremely heavy one. The Supreme Court has ruled that a defendant has no right to question jurors specifically about the contents of publicity they may have read or heard prior to trial. Not surprisingly, cases in which convictions have actually been set aside on the basis of prejudicial pretrial publicity are rare.

Can anything be done to combat prosecutorial bias in a particular case?

Sometimes. If a law is being enforced to discriminate against someone because of race, the defendant is entitled to have the prosecution dismissed on the grounds of selective enforcement. This doctrine was developed in a famous case decided in 1886 involving two Chinese laundrymen, Yick Wo and Wo Lee.

They were convicted of violating a San Francisco ordinance that required all laundries to be located in buildings of brick or stone. Their laundries were in wooden buildings. The ordinance was strictly enforced against Chinese—but not against members of other racial or ethnic groups who also ran laundries. The Court concluded that no reason for the prosecutions existed except hostility to the Chinese race and nationality. Under the circumstances, the convictions were unconstitutional. The Court held that even if a law is impartial on its face and is capable of being administered in a fair manner, "yet, if it is applied and administered by public authority with an evil eye and an unequal hand, so as practically to make unjust and illegal discriminations between persons in similar circumstances . . . the denial of equal justice is still within the prohibition of the Constitution."[3]

Is it difficult to prove selective enforcement of the law?

Yes. The facts showing "an evil eye and an unequal hand" are not usually as stark as they were in Yick Wo's case. The courts have also held that merely because the prosecution exercises some selectivity in enforcing the law does not establish a constitutional violation.

Will the federal courts ever prohibit state court prosecutions or expunge the record of convictions on the grounds of discriminatory, selective enforcement?

Yes, but only in the most limited of circumstances. Generally, federal courts refuse to interfere with state criminal proceedings because of the doctrines of "comity" (respect for state court functions), "equity" (avoiding a duplication of legal proceedings), and "federalism" (recognition of the fact that the country is a union of separate state governments).

During the early days of the civil-rights movement, federal

141

courts occasionally enjoined, or prohibited, state proceedings where the law was clearly being enforced in a discriminatory manner, as in the case of Yick Wo. However, the Supreme Court has more recently held that when federal courts are asked to enjoin state proceedings, normally they must refuse. The only exception is where the state prosecution amounts to bad faith or harassment.

Do federal courts have the power to enjoin federal officials from following a deliberate policy of discriminatory investigations and prosecutions?

Yes. One court, for example, held that it would violate the Constitution for the attorney general of the United States and other Department of Justice officials to investigate and prosecute blacks simply to deprive them of the right to vote.

Is there any way to remove state prosecutions to the federal courts to protect constitutional rights?

Yes. Federal law provides that any civil or criminal action in a state court may be removed to federal court if the defendant is denied or cannot enforce in the state court a right protected by federal law. The federal courts, however, have made it extremely difficult to remove cases because of their concern over increasing the caseload in federal court and their reluctance to interfere in state criminal proceedings. As a practical matter, the only cases that can be removed are those in which a defendant has a right not even to be brought to trial in the state court. In a 1966 case, for example, the Supreme Court allowed the removal of state prosecutions of blacks charged with trespass because of their sit-in demonstrations at a restaurant in Atlanta, Georgia. The Court held that the Civil Rights Act of 1964 granted an absolute right not to be prosecuted for seeking access to public accommodations.

9

FEDERAL CRIMINAL STATUTES PROTECTING THE RIGHTS OF MINORITIES

One of the most melancholy chapters in the history of race relations in the United States involves the failure of the criminal law to protect the lives and property of minorities. That failure was a predictable consequence of racial exclusion in the justice system discussed earlier. It was also the consequence of an entire way of life that valued people differently according to the color of their skin. The law, no matter what its theory, in practice worked first and always to protect the rights of whites. Only thereafter, if at all, did it protect the rights of minorities.

Racial violence and terrorism, the ultimate forms of discrimination, have been rampant and often unchecked by the normal operation of state criminal laws. During the 1880s and 1890s, for example, there were about 100 reported lynchings of blacks every year in the United States. In 1892 there were 155. Lynchings continued briskly over the next twenty years. There were 75 in 1909, 80 in 1910, 63 in 1911, and rarely less than 50 per year from then until 1923. During the height of the civil-rights movement from 1956 to 1965, there were 80 race-related killings. In Mississippi during the summer of 1964 alone there were reports of racial violence involving 35 shootings, 30 bombings, 35 church-burnings, and at least 6 murders.

RECONSTRUCTION-ERA CRIMINAL STATUTES

Are there any federal criminal statutes that protect minorities against racial violence and other forms of discrimination?

Yes. Congress enacted a law in 1866 making it a crime for any person acting "under color of law" willfully to deprive another of any right protected by the Constitution or laws of the United States by reason of color or race. Those convicted may be punished by fine of up to $1,000 or imprisonment for up to life.

Four years later, in 1870, Congress enacted a statute to curb the terrorist activities of white supremacist organizations such as the Ku Klux Klan and the Knights of the White Camellia, which had become increasingly active during the post–Civil War years. The law prohibits conspiracies by two or more persons to injure or intimidate any citizen in the exercise of any right protected by federal law. The statute also prohibits persons from wearing masks or disguises with the intent of preventing others from exercising their rights. Those convicted may be punished by a fine of up to $10,000 or imprisoned for up to life.

What does "under color of law" mean in the 1866 law?

"Under color of law" means that the wrongdoer is acting with the authority of law. For example, a law-enforcement officer who turns a prisoner over to a lynch mob is acting under color of law. Acts can be done under color of law even though they may be themselves violations of the law.

144

Are private individuals subject to prosecution under the 1866 law?

Yes, if they act under color of law or engage in criminal conduct with others who act under color of law. In one case, for instance, in 1964, several private individuals conspired with the sheriff and deputy sheriff of Neshoba County, Mississippi, to murder three civil-rights workers—James Chaney, Andrew Goodman, and Michael Schwerner. As part of the conspiracy, law-enforcement officers arrested the three and released them from the county jail after dark. A group of men (including the sheriff, the deputy, and the private individuals) later waylaid the rights workers on a lonely road, took them from their car, murdered them, and buried their bodies in a remote earthen dam. All of the conspirators were tried in federal court and found to be acting under color of law. The deputy and six others were convicted and sentenced to six years in prison for depriving Chaney, Goodman, and Schwerner of their civil rights. There were never any convictions in state court for murder or any other crime under state law.

Is action under color of law also required for prosecution of conspiracies under the 1870 statute?

No. Congress has the power to punish all conspiracies that interfere with constitutional rights, whether or not the conspirators are acting under color of state law. Thus, a purely private conspiracy to deprive someone of his or her civil rights can be prosecuted under the statute.

Are all acts of racial discrimination federal crimes?

No. Only those that are "willful" and deprive a person of some right expressly protected by federal law are criminal under the 1866 and 1870 laws. Willfulness means that a person acted with the specific purpose of depriving another of a protected right.

145

What kind of acts are punishable under the two federal laws?

A wide variety, including interfering with the following rights: to vote; to perfect a homestead; of federal officers to perform their duties; to be free from involuntary servitude and slavery; to attend school without regard to race or color; to participate in a civil-rights protest march; to equal protection under the Fourteenth Amendment; to full enjoyment of public accommodations; to interstate travel; and to trial by jury.

Have the federal laws been effectively enforced?

Generally, no. Immediately after the Civil War, the federal government made a concerted effort to enforce civil-rights laws protecting minorities. Prosecutions were brought against persons interfering with the rights of blacks to vote in congressional elections and to be secure in their persons and property. However, only about 20 percent of all prosecutions resulted in convictions, while courts severely limited the application of the federal statutes.

From the turn of the century until 1939, the enforcement of the two laws declined dramatically. Only four cases involving the laws reached the Supreme Court during this period.

In 1939, Congress established a civil-rights section in the Department of Justice and directed it to pursue a program of vigorous enforcement of civil rights. More prosecutions were brought under the federal laws than during prior years. The Supreme Court upheld charges against election officials who made a fraudulent count of the votes and who stuffed ballot boxes in federal elections. But the federal policy of enforcement was for the most part cautious and restrained, designed, according to the Justice Department, to avoid interfering with the administration of local criminal laws by state courts.

CRIMINAL STATUTES PROHIBITING SLAVERY, INVOLUNTARY SERVITUDE, AND PEONAGE

Has Congress made slavery, involuntary servitude, and peonage criminal activities?

Yes. Congress enacted criminal statutes after the Civil War prohibiting slavery, involuntary servitude (compulsory service of one person to another), and peonage (involuntary servitude with the added factor of indebtedness of one person to another). Punishments for violations of the laws include fines of up to $10,000 and imprisonment for up to five years.

Are slavery, involuntary servitude, and peonage widespread practices today?

Slavery and involuntary servitude, except in a few isolated cases, no longer exist in this country. Forcing a person to work to pay off a debt was fairly common during the years following the Civil War and was often little more than a substitute for slavery. Federal officials did not aggressively enforce the peonage law, and many states enacted laws making it a crime for a person to quit work if he owed money to his employer. As a consequence, the Immigration Commission in 1910 reported that cases of probable peonage had been found in all but two states in the Union. Maine had the most complete system of peonage in the entire country in its lumber camps.

Courts eventually struck down state laws that made it a crime for a person to fail to perform work for which he had been paid. In one of these cases, decided in 1944, the Supreme Court reversed the conviction of a black laborer who had received a five-dollar advance but failed to do the promised work. The states are free to punish fraud, the Court said, but no state can make quitting a job a component of a crime, or allow a person to hold another in peonage. The employer's remedy was a suit for breach of contract. Instances of peonage are still occasionally reported, mainly involving crew chiefs who used physical force to hold migrant agricultural workers in labor camps.

Are there forms of compulsory service that are constitutional?

Yes. The draft, civilian labor as an alternative to military service, jury duty, and hard labor pursuant to a lawful prison sentence have all been held not to violate the Thirteenth Amendment's ban on slavery and involuntary servitude. Curt Flood, a major-league baseball player, argued in a 1972 case that the league's system allowing players to be "sold" to other teams was a form of involuntary servitude. The court rejected the argument on the ground that Flood was free not to play baseball at all.

MODERN CRIMINAL STATUTES

Has there been any modern federal legislation imposing criminal penalties for interference with minority rights?

Yes. Congress enacted the Civil Rights Act of 1968 and provided criminal penalties for willful interference by force or threat of force with certain rights and activities. The statute prohibits anyone, whether or not acting under color of law, from injuring or interfering with one who has voted, campaigned for office, or qualified as an election official; participated in any federal program; applied for or secured federal employment; served as a grand or trial juror; or participated in any program receiving federal assistance. The statute also prohibits racial discrimination in public schools and colleges; in state programs; in employment by states, private individuals, or labor unions; in jury duty; in interstate commerce; and in public accommodations. Persons who interfere with interstate commerce during riot or civil disorder are also subject to prosecution, as are those who intimidate others participating in speech and assembly opposing racial discrimination. The penalties for violation of the statute are a fine of up to $10,000 or imprisonment for up to life.

Has the 1968 law been effectively enforced?

Only partially. The sweep of the law appears to be great, but a number of provisions restrict its use. No prosecution may be undertaken unless the attorney general states in writing that it is in the public interest and necessary to secure substantial justice. No law-enforcement officer is in violation of the statute for lawfully carrying out official duties or enforcing the laws of the United States or any state. The government has the burden of proving willfulness and the use of force or threat of force.

Given these restrictions and the comity (respect for state functions) that the federal government normally pays to state law enforcement, there have been relatively few prosecutions for violations of the statute. Successful prosecutions, however, have been brought against those who interfered with civil-rights demonstrators, denied minorities the use and enjoyment of public accommodations, blocked efforts by a civil-rights organization to promote employment and housing opportunities for blacks, and impeded the ability of blacks to attend desegregated schools.

Has Congress taken any other action in response to acts of discrimination and intimidation against racial and other minority groups?

Yes. Congress enacted the Hate Crimes Statistics Act of 1990 to establish a national data-collection system to compile statistics concerning bias-related crimes. The act requires the attorney general to publish an annual summary of the findings to be used for research and statistical purposes.

What should a person do who believes that someone has committed an act made a crime by federal laws prohibiting racial discrimination?

Notify the Department of Justice, Washington, D.C., or the department's nearest local office, and request that it investigate the incident for possible violations of federal law. The state prosecutor should also be notified, since the incident may involve violations of state law as well.

STATE LAWS PROHIBITING RACIAL DISCRIMINATION

Do the states also have criminal laws prohibiting discrimination based upon race?

Yes. Almost every state has laws making it a crime to discriminate against persons because of their race. These laws are frequently referred to as hate-crime laws.

The older state laws were aimed at white terrorist groups. They prohibited such things as wearing a mask, burning a cross, "Kukluxing" (making intimidating and threatening statements), and desecrating a religious place of worship. More recent laws have been enacted in response to an increase in bias-motivated crimes. Some make specific acts of racial discrimination unlawful, such as a conspiracy to deprive someone of his or her civil rights. Others increase the punishment for already existing crimes committed with a racially discriminatory intent.

Have state hate-crime laws been held constitutional?

Yes, where they punish conduct as opposed to speech. The supreme court of Georgia, for example, ruled that its law prohibiting wearing a mask was constitutional. The law allowed exceptions for people wearing holiday costumes, a gas mask in a fire drill, and so forth.

The Supreme Court of the United States held a Wisconsin law constitutional that increased the penalty for aggravated battery from two to seven years where the accused selected his victim because of race. The Court concluded that bias-motivated crimes inflicted greater individual and societal harm (emotional harm to the victim and unrest to the community), thereby justifying a more severe penalty.

But in another case, decided in 1992 and involving the city of St. Paul, Minnesota, the Court reversed the conviction of a white teenager who burned a cross in the yard of a black family in violation of a city ordinance. The ordinance made it a crime to place an object on public or private property which aroused anger or resentment in others on the basis of race, religion, or gender. While acknowledging that the defendant might have violated state laws prohibiting conduct such as arson and damage to property, the Court found the ordinance unconstitutional because it only prohibited the use of objects that aroused anger or resentment. The Court viewed the ordinance as being based on the content of speech and as a form of censorship. The cross-burning case is controversial because it involves fundamental but competing interests—a state's interest in prohibiting racial discrimination and the right of free speech that lies at the heart of our democratic system. Reconciling these interests is often a very difficult task.

If an act is a violation of both federal and state criminal laws, may it be prosecuted by both governments?

Yes. When an act is made a crime by both federal and state governments, it is a separate offense to the peace and dignity of each and may be punished as such. However, the Department of Justice has a policy of not prosecuting individuals tried in state court for federal offenses involving the same acts. Exceptions can be made, but only for compelling reasons and only with the approval of the attorney general.

10

RACE-CONSCIOUS REMEDIES

Legislatures, courts, and the American public have recognized that the country's long history of discrimination often makes remedial race-conscious programs necessary. Race-conscious programs enable members of minority groups to enter various areas—in employment or education, for example—from which they have been excluded previously through discrimination. Race-conscious measures are attempts to ensure that all Americans are treated as equal citizens, and to achieve equal opportunity that is truly open to all.

What are race-conscious strategies?

In the broadest sense, whenever race is specifically used to design or implement a program, there is a race-conscious strategy. In the effort to overcome racial discrimination and to achieve cultural diversity, many schools, employers, and other institutions have used programs designed to bring more minorities into the classroom and the workplace. These race-conscious strategies recognize that for generations minorities have been denied an opportunity to participate as equals in the political, social, cultural, and economic life of this country. Although formal state enforcement of segregation and other legal barriers to equal opportunity have been abandoned in the past 30 years, the legacy of discrimination is all too evident today.

What are some examples of race-conscious strategies?

Some of the strategies that are most familiar in our society are school desegregation plans, voting redistricting to increase minority participation, affirmative action, and business set-aside programs.

How are race-conscious strategies used?

Most race-conscious remedies adopt two main strategies. First, an attempt is made to expand the pool of applicants from the group that is underrepresented. The second strategy is to give the underrepresented group special consideration in the allocation of benefits.

Can the problem of excluding minorities be entirely addressed by removing the legal barrier that excluded minorities?

No. Although this is an important part of overcoming the past practice of discrimination and exclusion, it is not enough. Even without legal barriers to equal participation, discrimination continues to exist in our society. As Supreme Court Justice Lewis Powell noted on a number of occasions, we cannot undo the legacy of racial discrimination simply by repealing laws. Race must be taken into account affirmatively, in order to overcome racism.

Who benefits from affirmative-action programs?

Everyone. A society that is free of invidious racial discrimination or the effects of such discrimination celebrates our diversity and benefits the entire society.

Why is it necessary to consider race? Isn't the best way to overcome racism to ignore race as a factor?

In order to remedy the effects of past discrimination, race must be taken into account. Properly tailored remedial measures are efforts to achieve a social situation in which individuals are evaluated on their individual abilities, rather than as a product of their race.

In many areas where intentional racial discrimination once existed, minorities remain significantly underrepresented and face disproportionately difficult challenges in achieving success. First, many employers who used discriminatory practices in the past maintain a biased candidate profile which they used in making hiring decisions. Second, these employers have discriminatory reputations in minority communities that discourage minorities from applying for jobs with them. Third, most employers, despite protestations of nondiscrimination, continue to recruit potential employees by word of mouth. This practice works to the advantage of friends and relatives of most employers' predominantly white workforces, and thus to the disadvantage of minorities who are not yet inside this word-of-mouth system. In order to place disfavored persons in a position of equal footing, institutions seek, or may be required, to consider minority applicants.

Do some race-conscious programs, like affirmative action, require unqualified minority persons to be employed or promoted?

No. Affirmative action has never meant that a minority person who is not qualified must be given a job. Instead, affirmative action means that qualified minority persons must be recruited and fully considered for employment and promotion.

At the same time, affirmative action requires employers to look at how the word "qualifications" are used and what it means. First, employers have been forced to realize that, regardless of the advent of affirmative action, many persons have been hired or promoted not on the basis of job qualifications but on the basis of appearance, personality, club membership, and even friendship. Since the applicant who is theoretically best qualified is not necessarily the one who wins the job or the promotion, affirmative action simply requires that minority applicants, too, be fully considered. Second, and more important, employers have been forced to realize that many so-called qualifications are discriminatory devices unrelated to job performance. For example, many employers use culturally biased written tests which are not only discriminatory, but are also unable to predict job performance. Affirmative action requires employers to reexamine required qualifications, to recognize that many minority members who do not possess these are in fact qualified for employment and promotion, and thereby to include minority persons in the pool of qualified applicants.

An appropriate preference program does not abandon qualifications, but tries to ensure that qualifications used are related to performance. For these programs, racial-minority status serves as a positive factor along with other qualifications.

Can race-conscious numerical measures be adopted voluntarily by *private* employers without regard to past discrimination?

Yes. The Supreme Court has allowed plans adopted by private employers to remain in place without making the private employer prove a compelling need and a substantial amount of past discrimination. One form of a numerical measure is specific goals set by employers that attempt to diversify the workplace by recruiting and hiring a number of qualified minority applicants.

Are *government* programs that classify and treat people differently based on race a violation of the Fourteenth Amendment?

Not necessarily. Government programs that take race into account to correct the effects of past discrimination are distinguishable from programs that exclude some people from opportunities accorded to all citizens. The former strives to place disfavored persons in a position of equal footing, and the latter actively deprives people of equal footing. When past discrimination has been so bad and widespread that some people are deprived of equal opportunities, race must be taken into account to correct the discrimination.

Has the Supreme Court ruled on the constitutionality of affirmative action programs or in any way limited their use?

The Supreme Court has not found that affirmative action programs are, as a rule, unconstitutional. However, in a case originating in Colorado, *Adarand Constructors Inc. v. Pena* (1995), the Supreme Court narrowed the use of race-conscious programs by all government entities. As a result, local, state, and federal governments must follow strict guidelines in creating race-conscious remedies.

How did the Supreme Court narrow the use of affirmative-action programs?

The Court will examine race-conscious programs adopted by any government body under a standard called "strict scrutiny."

The *Adarand* case applied this standard to all levels of government. Under strict scrutiny, a governmental program that takes race into account to benefit certain groups must be for a "compelling," or very important, interest, and must be "narrowly tailored" to advance that interest. This standard is difficult but not impossible to meet.

What interests are compelling enough for a governmental body to enact race-conscious measures?

Pervasive and systematic discrimination is a compelling reason to enact race-conscious remedies. In such cases, race becomes a remedial or benign classification intended to correct harmful racial classifications. A mere claim of persistent discrimination, however, is not a sufficient basis for enacting a race-conscious remedy. Strong evidence of discriminatory conduct, usually including both statistical effects and specific observations, is necessary for a race-conscious measure to survive review by a court. In the past, the Supreme Court has recognized a compelling governmental interest in achieving racial diversity. A recent decision, however, indicates that a showing of actual discrimination may be necessary for the government interest to be compelling.

Does the use of a strict scrutiny standard mean that governmental bodies will not be able to have race-conscious affirmative-action programs?

No. Strictly scrutinizing race-conscious measures does not mean that all such measures violate constitutional equal-protection guarantees. The Supreme Court separates benign or remedial classifications from classifications that treat some groups as racially inferior. The Court thus recognizes that benign and remedial racial classifications can be constitutional, and indeed further the guarantee of equal protection by remedying the effects of past discrimination. Strict scrutiny is still a difficult standard to meet, and courts will require specific evidence that a racial classification is necessary when the government's claimed interest is to remedy past discrimination.

Is remedying past discrimination a "compelling" state interest that can justify a state or local government's adoption of an affirmative-action hiring plan?

Yes. The Court indicated in *City of Richmond v. J. A. Croson Co.* (1989) that the goal of remedying past discrimination would be considered "compelling" in order to justify a minority set-aside. However, the evidence of prior discrimination must be based on precise legislative findings and should show a strong case of a constitutional or statutory violation. The following factors would be enough to justify a set-aside:

(1) Where the government can prove the existence of discrimination by specific individuals or groups. The best possibility of satisfying this test is to show that the governmental body adopting the preference program is itself responsible for the past discrimination. Preferably, assertions of such discrimination should be backed up with written or oral descriptions by several people evidencing specific examples of the discrimination. Evidence of specific acts that form a pattern may be necessary.

(2) Where a governmental body can prove by inference that discrimination against a minority exists. A valid statistical inference of discrimination could be made from a showing that qualified minority firms are getting a substantially smaller percentage of work than other firms. For example, a relevant statistic would indicate how many Minority Business Enterprises (MBEs) in the relevant market (city, county, state) are qualified to undertake prime or subcontracting work in public construction projects. Similarly, the percentage of total city construction dollars that minority firms are receiving as subcontrac-

tors compared to the total dollars awarded would be relevant.

(3) Where the government has become a "passive participant" in a system of racial exclusion. For instance, a government's spending practices may compound discrimination by other governmental or private bodies. In this case, the government would have the authority to take affirmative steps to dismantle such a system.

What interests are *not* "compelling" enough to justify a set-aside?

The majority opinion in *Croson*, reaffirmed in *Adarand*, implies that the following justifications for affirmative action are not compelling:

(1) A set-aside designed to remedy the effects of general societal discrimination.

(2) Generalized assertions that there has been past discrimination in an entire industry. Such assertions do not provide guidance for determining the precise scope of the injury. Moreover, the remedy for such injuries is difficult to define, and may be too broad in relation to the actual injury.

(3) A mere recitation of a "benign" or legitimate purpose for the racial classification. This justification will be given "little or no weight," as will individual legislators' views that there has been past discrimination in the industry.

(4) Statistical comparisons between the actual percentage of minorities receiving contracts and the percentage of minorities in the general population. The Supreme Court has held that the relevant statistical pool for purposes of demonstrating discriminatory exclusion must be the number of minorities qualified to undertake the particular task.

(5) Findings of nationwide discrimination in the construction industry. This evidence was deemed extremely limited as a justification for a state/local government set-aside plan. Such a

finding is too broad to provide guidance of the actual injury or necessary remedy.

(6) The inclusion of minority groups in a set-aside program, where there has been no evidence that those particular groups have been disadvantaged. Such a justification suggests that the compelling interest is not in fact the remedying of past discrimination.

(7) The goal of achieving diversity in the workplace. Such a goal has been considered an "important," but not a "compelling" interest.

A government entity that wants to adopt a race-conscious program must have a compelling interest in doing so. Once it has satisfied this requirement, will its program be constitutional?

Not necessarily. The program must meet a second requirement that it be narrowly tailored to achieve the intended results of remedying specific past discrimination.

How have the courts approached set-aside programs since *Croson*?

A number of lower court cases following *Croson* have found affirmative-action plans to be constitutional. Federal courts have indicated that to be constitutionally valid, an affirmative-action plan must meet four basic requirements:

(1) Show sufficient factual evidence to justify the set-aside plan;

(2) Present evidence that the state or local government has considered race-neutral plans as alternatives to the set-aside plan;

(3) Tie the percentage preference contained in the set-aside plan to the availability of qualified minority contractors; and

(4) Show that the set-aside plan contains a provision

161

where the minority preference may be waived or reduced if qualified MBEs are not available or if a bidding MBE's higher price is not a result of past discrimination.

Written or oral descriptions by actual people demonstrating past discrimination in the industry can be very persuasive. Evidence should apply directly to the industry within the particular jurisdiction, as opposed to general "societal discrimination." Some courts have interpreted *Croson* to mean that governmental entities can only remedy discrimination that has taken place within their jurisdictional boundaries. In addition to anecdotal evidence, statistical data on minority businesses will also be necessary. These figures should indicate that specific groups, such as blacks or women, who are qualified to work in the industry under consideration, have been underrepresented as recipients of government contracts.

Courts respond more favorably to affirmative-action plans that include a waiver provision allowing an employer or contractor to escape complying with the plan in certain circumstances. For example, courts indicate that if an employer shows that qualified women or minorities are not available, it should not be forced to comply with the plan. Similarly, courts respond favorably to waivers that allow an employer to demonstrate its good-faith effort to find qualified minorities or women for positions. Explicit waiver provisions should be included in the law enacting an affirmative-action plan.

How have the courts dealt with affirmative-action plans under Title VI and Title VIII of the Civil Rights Act, which prohibit discrimination in federally assisted programs and housing?

So far courts have rejected the application of *Croson* to such plans if the remedies stayed within the broad discretionary powers granted to housing authorities under these statutes. The recent *Adarand* decision applied strict scrutiny broadly, to include federal affirmative-action programs. Although it is unclear how courts will treat affirmative-action plans under Title VI or Title VIII specifically, any such government program now requires a compelling government interest and narrow tailoring to be found constitutional. Thus, if the federal government can demonstrate past discrimination in housing with sufficient evidence and that its remedial program is narrowly tailored, a federal affirmative-action plan in housing may survive strict scrutiny.

How have the courts dealt with affirmative-action in the area of education?

Determining what standard to apply to affirmative-action educational plans has proven to be a difficult task. For plans adopted pursuant to school desegregation litigation, it seems clear that *Croson* should not apply because of the court's broad remedial power in these cases and the existence of federal legislation in this area.

The more difficult issue in education arises when a school (or school district or state) has based its affirmative-action plan on its interest in something other than remedying the effects of past discrimination. In the *Bakke* case, the Court held that a "diverse student body" contributing to a "robust exchange of ideas" is a constitutionally permissible goal on which race-conscious university admissions programs may be based.

Whether such "nonremedial" objectives will be sufficient for state and local governments to bring their educational affirmative action programs outside the reach of *Croson* or *Adarand* is unclear at this time.

To what extent can a governmental program that considers race as a factor in giving preferential treatment for certain groups burden nonbenefited groups, without encroaching on equal-protection guarantees of the Constitution?

Supreme Court Justice Lewis Powell has stated that "as a part of this Nation's dedication to eradicating racial discrimination, innocent persons may be called upon to bear some of the burden of the remedy."[1] However, the remedy cannot *unduly* burden innocent persons, or it risks violating the equal protection provision of the Constitution. The Supreme Court has held, for example, that a race-conscious remedy that includes laying off existing employees places too great a burden on specific individuals, rather than diffusing the burden across the population. Less burdensome means, such as hiring goals, are more likely to pass constitutional muster.

NOTES

Decisions of the federal courts are contained in multivolume sets of books known as the Federal Supplement (abbreviated "F.Supp.") for the district courts, the Federal Reporter (abbreviated "F.," "F.2d.," or "F.3d") for the courts of appeals, and United States Reports (abbreviated "U.S.") or Supreme Court Reports (abbreviated "S.Ct.") for the Supreme Court. The names of the parties involved in the case come first, next the volume number, next the name of the reporter, next the page on which the case begins, next the name of the court, and finally the date of the decision. For example, 376 F.Supp. 750 (M.D.Fla. 1974) means that the case appears in volume 376 of the Federal Supplement on page 750 and was decided by the district court for the middle district of Florida in 1974. The librarian at a law school or a library that has law books can help you locate any of the decisions that are cited in this book. The decisions are also available online through Westlaw and Lexis, and through the World Wide Web.

Chapter 1

1. 60 U.S. (19 How.) 393, 407 (1857).
2. *The Souls of Black Folk* 10 (1989).
3. 347 U.S. 483, 495 (1954).

Chapter 2

1. S. Rep. No. 417, 97th Cong., 2d Sess. 34 (1982).

Chapter 4

1. 347 U.S. 483 (1954).
2. 418 U.S. 717 (1974).
3. 115 S.Ct. 2038 (1995).
4. 438 U.S. 265 (1978).

Chapter 5

1. 392 U.S. 409, 413 (1968).
2. *Metropolitan Housing Development Co. v. Village of Arlington Heights*, 558 F.2d 1283, 1290 (7th Cir 1977).

Chapter 6

1. *Plessy v. Ferguson*, 163 U.S. 537, 16 S.Ct. 1138, 1143 (1896).
2. *Brown v. Board of Education*, 347 U.S. 483, 495 (1954).

CHAPTER 7

1. 110 Cong. Rec. 6544.
2. *Young v. Pierce*, 628 F. Supp. 1037, 1056 (E.D. Tex. 1985).

CHAPTER 8

1. *Strauder v. West Virginia*, 100 U.S. 303, 308 (1880).
2. *Moore v. Dempsey*, 251 U.S. 86, 91 (1923).
3. *Yick Wo v. Hopkins*, 118 U.S. 356, 373–74 (1886).

CHAPTER 10

1. *Wygant v. Jackson Board of Education*, 476 U.S. 267, 280–81 (1986).

RESOURCES

FOR FURTHER READING

Nonfiction

An American Dilemma: The Negro Problem and Modern Democracy by Gunnar Myrdal. New York: Harper, 1944. A Swedish economist writes about the contradictions between America's ideals and its racial practices.

Asian American: Chinese and Japanese in the U.S. Since 1850 by Roger Daniels. Seattle: University of Washington Press, 1988. A history of Asians in the United States.

Bury My Heart at Wounded Knee by Dee Brown. New York: Holt, Rinehart & Winston, 1971. The story of westward expansion told from the Native American point of view.

Days of Grace: A Memoir by Arthur Ashe. New York: Knopf, 1993. A moving account by the world-class tennis player of his life and, finally, his struggle with AIDS.

Having Our Say: The Delany Sisters' First 100 Years by

Sarah and A. Elizabeth Delany. New York: Kodansha International, 1993. Living history told by two ancient, spirited, irreverent, and persevering black sisters who knew just about everybody who was anybody in black America between the turn of the century and the 1980s.

From Slavery to Freedom: A History of Negro Americans by John Hope Franklin and Alfred A. Moses, Jr. New York: McGraw-Hill, 1988. A classic account of the struggle for racial freedom and dignity.

The Indispensable Enemy: Labor and the Anti-Chinese Movement in California by Alexander Saxton. Berkeley: University of California Press, 1971. A history of the exploitation of Chinese labor in California.

Life and Times of Frederick Douglass by Frederick Douglass. London: Collier Books, 1962. The autobiography by the ex-slave, who became an abolitionist and the greatest African-American leader of the nineteenth century.

Notes of a Native Son by James Baldwin. Boston: Beacon Press, 1955. A collection of lively essays that take the author from Harlem to Paris.

Letter from the Birmingham Jail by Martin Luther King, Jr. San Francisco: Harper, 1994. The leader of the modern civil-rights movement writes about civil disobedience.

Margins and Mainstreams: Asians in American History and Culture by Gary Y. Okihiro. Seattle: University of Washington Press, 1994. An update on the Asian-American experience.

Mexican Americans: Leadership, Ideology, and Identity, 1930–1960 by Mario T. Garcia. New Haven: Yale University Press, 1989. A study of Mexican Americans.

The Mind of the South by W. J. Cash. New York: Random House, 1941. A white Southern journalist takes a critical look at the mind and myths of the South.

Soul on Ice by Eldridge Cleaver. New York: Dell, 1968.

Reflections of a former leader of the Black Panthers.

The Souls of Black Folk by W.E.B. DuBois. New York: Modern Library, 1996. A black intellectual prophesies that the problem of the twentieth century will be the color line.

The Strange Career of Jim Crow by C. Vann Woodward. New York: Oxford University Press, 1957. A history of racial segregation in the South.

Strangers from a Different Shore: A History of Asian Americans by Ronald Takaki. Boston: Little, Brown, 1989. A comprehensive history of the Asian-American experience.

Up from Slavery: An Autobiography by Booker T. Washington. New York: Doubleday, Page & Co., 1902. The autobiography of the former president of Tuskegee Institute and one of the foremost African-American leaders of his day.

Walls and Mirrors: Mexican Americans, Mexican Immigrants, and the Politics of Ethnicity by David G. Gutierrez. University of California Press, 1995. A comprehensive history of Mexican Americans.

Novels, plays, videos, and poems

The Adventures of Huckleberry Finn by Mark Twain. Huck, a young white boy, and Jim, a runaway slave, raft down the Mississippi River in search of adventure and freedom. Many editions available.

The Bluest Eye by Toni Morrison. New York: Holt, Rinehart and Winston, 1970. Fiction by a celebrated award-winning African-American writer.

Fires in the Mirror by Anna Deavere Smith. Alexandria: PBS Video, 1993. Sharply drawn portraits based on interviews about the racial violence in Crown Heights, Brooklyn, in 1991.

Invisible Man by Ralph Ellison. New York: Random House,

1947. A black man's search for identity in a segregated society.

Ma Rainey's Black Bottom by August Wilson. Pittsburgh: University of Pittsburgh Press, 1991. One of Wilson's most popular plays, and a sharp criticism of white racial attitudes.

Native Son by Richard Wright. New York: Harper & Row, 1940. The tragic story of Bigger Thomas, a young black man hardened by life in the slums of Southside Chicago.

A Raisin in the Sun by Lorraine Hansberry. New York: Modern Library, 1995. A play about the betrayal of the American dream.

Selected Poems by Rita Dove. New York: Vintage Books, 1993. A collection of poems by a Pulitzer-prize-winning African-American author.

ORGANIZATIONS

These national and regional organizations provide support for racial and ethnic groups in Congress, state and local governments, and in the courts. Some of them have newsletters and other publications that you can order or receive by becoming a member.

American Civil Liberties Union
125 Broad Street
New York, NY 10004
(212) 549-2500

Asian Law Caucus
468 Bush Street
San Francisco, CA 94108
(415) 391-1655

Indian Law Resource Center
602 North Ewing Street
Helena, MT 59601
(406) 449-2006

Lawyers Committee for Civil Rights under Law
1400 I Street, N.W.
Washington, D.C. 20005
(202) 371-1212

Mexican American Legal Defense and
Educational Fund
634 S. Spring Street
Los Angeles, CA 90014
(213) 629-2512

NAACP Legal Defense and
Educational Fund, Inc.
99 Hudson Street
New York, NY 10013
(212) 219-1900

National Association for the Advancement
of Colored People
4805 Mount Hope Drive
Baltimore, MD 21215
(301) 358-8900

Native American Rights Fund
1506 Broadway
Boulder, CO 80302
(303) 447-8760

Puerto Rican Legal Defense and Education Fund
99 Hudson Street
New York, NY 10013
(212) 219-3360

Southwest Voter Registration Education Project
403 E. Commerce Street
San Antonio, TX 78205
(512) 222-0224

INDEX

A

Ability tests used in hiring process, 39
Adarand Constructors v. Pena, 157–58
Affirmative action, 154–64
    Adarand Constructors v. Pena, 157–58
    in educational admissions, 70–73, 163
    in employment, 45–50
    set asides, *see* Set asides
AIDS, 80
Air travel, discrimination in, 99
American Dilemma, An (Myrdal), 5
Anti–single shot laws, 19
Armed forces, desegregation of, 5
At-large elections, 17, 29, 31
Attorney general, U.S., 82–83, 114

B

Back-pay awards, 43–44

Laughlin McDonald is a graduate of Columbia University and the University of Virginia Law School. He has been director of the Southern Regional Office of the American Civil Liberties Union in Atlanta, Georgia, since 1972. He has represented minorities in numerous discrimination cases, testified frequently before Congress, and has written extensively for scholarly and popular publications on constitutional and civil liberties issues.

john a. powell is presently a professor at the University of Minnesota Law School and director of the Institute on Race and Poverty. He is also a consultant on minority and consumer rights in Africa. He previously served as national legal director of the American Civil Liberties Union. Before coming to the ACLU, powell taught law at the University of San Francisco Law School and practiced housing law.